The Coven of the Scales

The Collected Writings of Bob Clay-Egerton

compiled by
Mélusine Draco

First published in Great Britain as a
Collection by ignotus press 2002
from material already in the public domain

BCM-Writer, London WC1N 3XX

British Library Cataloguing in Publication Data
ISBN: 1 903768 04 7

Edited by Claire Maguire
Illustrations: A R Clay-Egerton
Printed in Great Britain by A2 Reprographics
Set in Baskerville Old Face 11pt

Contents

Foreword

In the short time since his death, the reputation of Alastair 'Bob' Clay-Egerton has begun to pass into pagan legend alongside other contemporary characters such as Robert Cochrane and Bill Gray. There are numerous people who can lay claim to having worked with him – from those whose acquaintance was confined to a single public ritual, to those who trained with him over a long period of time. Everyone has a favourite 'Bob' story which demonstrates his eccentricity or, more often than not, the speed of the put-down for those who insisted on making public idiots of themselves. Few knew him on an inner magical level.

For this reason it is extremely difficult to describe his type of magical teaching except to say that, from personal experience, the student flew by the seat of their pants – often at a horrifying rate of knots! This collection of viewpoints, opinions and perspectives were published under a variety of names, depending on the subject matter and only represent a very small percentage of his prodigious outpourings. The bulk of the magical writings were penned by Alastair Clay-Egerton; the downright confrontational material by the greatly loved 'old devil' himself, Asmodaeus, while the wind-up pieces came from the 'Spoonwielder'.

As he often said: "It may well be thought, and even said that, 'Here is Asmodaeus stirring up strife and dissention again', but this is not my intention. Actually, it is never my intention to stir up discord for the sake of discord. I merely wish to make people *think,* to stir up mental lethargy, to kick the complacent, and hope that we might all learn something in the process."

Whenever possible, Bob speaks for himself and only the occasional editing of his writing has been carried out for the purpose of clarity and continuity. There is much, much more out there in the public domain that, if it were all collected together, would make up several bulky tomes. It is hoped that newcomers to the world of magical practice will gain some valuable insights into the ways of Old Craft (i.e. pre-Garderian) and, even if they may not agree with them, may go away with points to ponder.

It is probably easier to say what Bob wasn't than what he was. He was most certainly *not* Wiccan, being a constant source of irritation to most of them and, despite having been chums with both Gerald Gardner and Alex Sanders, embraced neither Gardnerian nor Alexandrian traditions. A Warden of Alderley Edge, he was neither pacifist (being ex-military, as his writings often reveal), nor segregationist (having a practical understanding and respect for most religious beliefs and traditions). Both he and his wife, Mériém, were accomplished potholers, who formed one of the first cave rescue services, while Mériém herself held a Doctorate in Geology, with a strong working interest in archaeology and anthropology.

Bob was initiated into Old Craft back in 1941 and into a ritual magic order in 1943 but, contrary to popular belief, he neither knew Aleister Crowley, nor was he a member of either the Golden Dawn or the OTO. He *was* a member of the *Templi Satanas Luciferi* which, in modern parlance was a forerunner of the Tubal Cain-Luciferian tradition that is currently gaining in popularity. Mériém's background was Jewish with strong links towards Middle Eastern and Oriental philosophies. Their magical Order taught *all* these things without resorting to the popular pick-and-mix approach. Each philosophy or practice was dealt with and studied as a *separate* area and woe betide the student who tried to muddle Craft and Orientalism. There were three *separate* paths within the Order and the student followed whichever was suited to their own abilities or persuasions while retaining a healthy respect for the rest.

In Bob's own words: "Is it not time that we ceased to define things as being of East or West? All traditions, all thought, all innovations, come from One Source. It matters not whether they travel from North, South, East or West. All have validity and all have a common origin, even if we are not able to recognise this immediately. Impossible as it may seem at first without understanding, all Faiths are One."

Following this school of teaching, the student was able to study and work with those of other paths and traditions, without compromising their own faith or belief. It enabled them to converse with others from different philosophies on the subject of the 'tools' that were common to both and come to a greater understanding of occult principles from many differing viewpoints. As this book will show, there are many more facets to the Clay-Egertons' system of instruction than is generally taught by the majority of post-Wiccan groups who lay claim to ancient lineage or antecedents.

Neither was this discipline for the faint-hearted, often reflecting Bob and Mériém's own fearless pursuit of magical knowledge and experience. They taught and practised magic throughout the whole spectrum of 'forty shades of grey' and acceptance of this train of thought led to the 'scales' falling from the eyes of the seeker – then and only then, were they admitted to the Coven of the Scales. All who underwent Initiation into the Order will carry 'the mark' for the rest of their days.

There are no 'secrets' being given away here. Both Bob and Mériém, were prolific writers for the pagan press and this book is only a small selection of their magical thoughts and experiences that have appeared in print over many years. These extracts serve to give a brief glimpse into the all-encompassing occult teaching that was given to their students: the inner Mysteries will never appear in any book or publication. Neither will it be passed on to any who fail to achieve the level of practical working knowledge demanded by an Initiate of their Order.

In his closing years, Bob suffered from failing health, including a stroke which left him severely disabled until his death in 1998. Shortly before her own death, Mériém entrusted the bulk of Bob's papers into our safe keeping and, at the same time, formerly handed down his seal of the Esoteric Order of the Serpent. The Coven of the Scales and the EOS are still operational and continues to admit members whose magical skills echo the level and depth of magical exploration undertaken by both Bob and Mériém Clay-Egerton.

Mélusine Draco

A R Clay-Egerton

Devil's Advocate

Introduction

What causes us to write articles for occult magazines? Are we the recipients of illumination as a blinding light of insight directed at us by a god? Are we writing as the result of gentle absorption of knowledge received via a goddess? Or are we prodded into action by the business end of a demonic pitchfork?

Certainly not for financial gain; the alleged *news*papers would be far better enhancers of our bank balances. The financial aspect does come into it to some extent, I suppose. For example, I don't think I have ever purchased a copy of *Sirius* for years, If the equipment on which the magazine is produced has been updated, it is no thanks to *my* monetary subscriptions. I assure a steady supply of magazines as complimentary copies. This I do by supplying a stream of writings, under my demonic name, or my more socially acceptable one, or both. The hard work devolves upon the editors, who have the unenviable task of deciphering my hand written work – or my typing. They also have to cope with my spelling, punctuation and grammar, or lack of it.

Apart from requiring free copies of occult magazines, the real payment is probably the ego-boost of getting into print. After almost half a century, you might think the ego had been boosted enough. In addition to a slight pecuniary advantage and the elevation of the ego at appearing in print, there is the associated boost of fondly imagining that one's writings may actually do some good. That they may strike a responsive chord in someone's mind. That they may cause someone to *think for themselves.* Even if only to think what a twittle-head the author is.

The subjects for articles usually come unbidden from nowhere, before being prepared for infliction upon the public. The originating thoughts, to say nothing of the subsequent development, may be a manifestation of some divine entity. Is it always from a divine entity, however? When Frater Asmodaeus puts pen to paper (or finger to typewriter), it is usual for the content to appear as if intended to stir up strife and discord. Witchcraft becomes bitchcraft. Few seem to be safeguarded from the scorpion's strike. Such articles are usually written under the name of this fraternal demon.

But the term 'demon' had its origin in the Greek word *daemon* and this originally did not mean an evil entity. The word originally meant 'intelligence' or 'spirit'. An intelligence or spirit many not, of course, be always benign but by no means is it always evil. A daemon is more than likely to commence as neutral. Intelligences may breed intelligences; spirits may give birth to spirits. Let us stir up contention by considering this.

Humans have intelligence. True, the majority of humans appear to be devoid of it, or to have little experience in its constructive utilisation. You disagree? Before you rush into judgement, look around you. Consider for a moment the 'wonders' the use of man's intelligence has bequeathed to the world. The extinction of various species of animal, bird and insect. The pollution of the oceans, rivers and streams. The destruction of the ozone layer. The cultivation of biological mutations (my own children among them), by nuclear 'accidents and covered up for years for political reasons. Drugs produced for profit. Man's intelligence has produced, not better, but more destructive weapons of war.

This is intelligence? If it is, then the modern meaning attributed to the word daemon is correct, for if the intelligence or spirit of man can only accomplish these things, then it is certainly evil and destructive. Self-destructive!

But intelligence breeds intelligence; daemon breeds daemon. Man creates not just harmful artefacts but the thoughts which evolve them into tangible thought form. Thought forms have long been created by men and women but the end to which they are put depend on their creators. Thus the daemon may be for good or ill and the direction it takes depends ultimately on the spirit of its creator. Even if that spirit is nudged by a deity, it has free will to accept or reject the direction in which it is nudged.

Which direction will you take now for your personal spirit and its creator. *Quo vadis daemonae*

Alastair R Clay-Egerton
26th April 1997

Devil's Advocate

According to Alastair (Bob) Clay-Egerton himself, in *What You Call Time*, what he knew about contemporary witchcraft came from three sources. His own experience dating from 1941; what he had been told of coven history; and what he had learned from other Old Crafters who contacted him over the years in response to his writings in occult magazines.

"When I became associated with witchcraft it was still illegal in Britain and a further decade before the Witchcraft Act was repealed. How then did people become involved in the Craft? Certainly it did not seem to be a matter of being passed over from one member of a family to another in the case of the coven I joined. Or those to which I was later introduced in Shropshire and North Wales. My introduction was probably unique and at a much earlier age than most. My membership subsequently cost me dear and certainly changed the course of my life."

Born into an upper-middle class background in 1930, the young man was intrigued by the furtive antics of a housemaid, whilst staying at a weekend retreat in a Cheshire beauty spot. Following her through the woods he expected her to meet with her lover but instead she merely joined a small group of people and after a while he lost interest and crept away. The next month he again followed the maid but this time he was caught watching them.

"Consternation reigned! The Craft was illegal, there was a war in progress, meetings of a clandestine nature were suspect and Father, because of his position, presumably had access to restricted information. It was decided that I be allowed to attend meetings but I was sworn to secrecy on the word of a gentleman—which in those days was worth something. In the spring of my 13th year I was initiated into the coven. I had quickly become aware that some of the Witches were also members of a separate magical order which met locally and was initiated into that in the summer of 1943."

Unfortunately, in 1947 his occult connections were discovered and he was threatened with disinheritance unless he gave up occult study; was confirmed into the Church of England; and gave names and addresses, dates and times of both witches and magicians. Having refused, the treat was carried out and his younger brother became the heir to the estate, although after the repeal of the Witchcraft Act there was some reconciliation with the family.

"It may well be that the majority of Witches centuries ago were peasants or of yeoman stock, although this seems to have changed later," he concluded. "My own coven, I was informed, had received an influx of members in the 1800s. The copper deposits in this part of Cheshire were to be exploited again and Welsh miners were imported from Powys Mine in Anglesey. In North Wales some coven members were quarrymen. I have since heard of a pre-Gardnerian coven whose male members were all flagstone miners, and it was said before them, there had been a coven there of lead miners."

One of Bob's pet hates was the restrictive approach followed by many modern Witches and Wiccans who still refuse to see the broader aspects of Craft practice and which, long-term, results in stultification. Neither had he any patience for those (*Pagan News* 1991) who were more concerned with labels rather than getting on with the job. A situation that still exists in the pagan community today ...

"The Wiccan who pontificates that one who performs Golden Dawn rituals, or has an interest in chaos magic is not and cannot be a pagan may well have had the benefit of having received a good education. It is very unfortunate that, if this is the case, such a Wiccan might be identified by a student of Islamic history as being in the same class as some of the early *mullahs*. The *mullahs* in question were also well educated and set themselves up as teachers, saying to the people: 'Come, we will explain the words of the Prophet to you and tell you how to distinguish Muslim from non-Muslim'. When this was reported to the Mohammad it is recorded in *Bukhari Hadith*, that he smiled and merely replied: '*Almahuma aksaru min akliehima*–Their education is greater than their sense.'

The nit-picking and critical Wiccan would be better employed worrying about her own state of understanding and practice of Wicca than about who can and cannot be accepted as a 'true Wiccan and not be only an occultist'. Despite the screams and shouts, weeping and wailing from self-proclaimed 'hereditary' witches, Wicca is a *modern* phenomena. Its rites and ceremonies are latter day creations, attached to age-old festival dates.

What is a Witch? From a dictionary definition, a Witch is a woman who practices the 'black arts', a sorcerer, a necromancer. The biblical Witch of Endor was employed by the Jewish King to use necromancy on his behalf. From this it would seem that traditionally there are no male Witches and that the major occupation of Witches was communion with the dead! Let us not, however, concern ourselves too much with the old meanings – meanings change with time.

The modern Witch claims that the religion of witchcraft is Wicca, meaning 'wise'. The Old English word for 'wise' is *wis*. The word Wicca is surely derived from the Old Saxon word meaning to twist, to turn, to bend. I have known a few alleged Witches who are excellent at twisting; many who try to turn anything they can to their own advantage; and not a few who seem to wish to practice mind-bending.

If there is one thing I *do* admire about modern Witches it is their ability to change–not their shapes but their opinions. The early copies of an authoritative magazine allegedly speaking for witchcraft *per se*, declared that black people could not be Witches. They could only be magicians. Similarly it was stated that homosexuals could not be true Witches. To quote one statement: 'We want no kinks in our circles'.

The views appear to have changed radically. Changed so much indeed, that the late (genuinely lamented by those who really knew and understood him – even if they disagreed with him) Alex Sanders is no longer openly vilified, but only sneered at in a light-hearted way by some of the 'leaders' of the witchcraft movement.

Unfortunately, to my mind, the witchcraft movement all too frequently resembles a bowel movement. I don't refer to its alternating appearance of being hard and intractable at times, and at others soft and gushing. I refer to the fact that, bearing in mind the oft stated Wiccan Rede, it stinks!

"An it harm none ... do as thou wilt" is what they profess. So what do they do? They proceed to harm people's feelings and reputations. They declare Satanists to be evil when they have less knowledge or understanding of Satanism than a Jewish mother has of the satisfaction of a non-Jewish mother watching her family tuck into a good helping of pork sausages. They upset the feelings of those who do not happen to follow their own particular interpretation of the Ways of the Witch.

The true Witch, to my mind, is not the one who postures, promulgates and preaches (usually with some pecuniary advantage attached somewhere), on what a Witch believes but one who practices what they see as witchcraft, no matter what others may say.

Let Wicca encompass *all* those of whatever path they follow, who truly see themselves as being Wicca. Let us not fight among ourselves; we have enough to do fighting off the fundies who seek to destroy not only our beliefs but, if necessary, us personally.

Are Wiccans really pagans? Are other occult paths pagan? It depends on what meaning we are going to accept for the term. An old meaning of the word referred to any non-Christain. Muslims were classed as pagans as well as followers of Satan. Until, that is, the Muslim countries achieved independence and struck oil. Now there's magic for you! Oil: wealth; welcome to the inter-faith community!

The occultists in general are still out in the cold, pariahs, the poor relations. What we *can do* is decide that all occultists are pagan, whatever their practices. No discrimination; let us all be classed as pagan for our own protection and to hell with our detractors. Let us be certain what is a pagan, even if Wiccans cannot agree on what is a Wiccan."

Although this article was written ten years ago, the pagan v. Wiccan debate still goes on unabated and, although many of the facets of the argument *have* changed, there is still hostility between the different factions. Although Bob expressed the opinion that a true Witch should follow his or her own path, his article omits the qualification that they should have a firm grounding in practical magic before going off to do their own thing. For this reason, the first series of articles reproduced here deal with the question of occult tools and regalia.

In the first, Bob discusses the different types of knife that can be used as an athame, other than the usual black-handled variety. He was a stickler for detail and expected his students to know precisely what they were doing and why they were doing it. Unlike many tutors – the result was more information than you could possibly assimilate, and woe betide you if you were caught waving something about and didn't know why you were waving it!

The knife or athame is, of course, the most important tool in the whole panoply of witchcraft regalia. This is a highly personal item that has been created from fire, earth, air and water–and imbued with the spirit or Will of its owner. Properly consecrated, it is the embodiment or extension of the soul of the Witch, and a focus for directing power. I would hate to think what Bob's reaction would have been to those who bring a carved *wooden* knife into the Circle! Here is his own explanation ....

KNOW THY WEAPONS

The Athame or Knife

"No, it's not going to be a smutty joke. It's just that many witches don't seem to know an athame from an ice-pick.

An athame is composed of two main parts–you can remember them as one passive (for the God) and the other active (for the Goddess); together they form the athame as the God and Goddess together form the new God. The passive portion is called the 'hilt' or the 'half', while the active part is the blade.

The haft may be of almost any material from wood to plastic, plain or moulded, or carved, or bound with wire or cord, etc., to give a better grip. The extreme end is called the 'butt' and may be squared off, angled, rounded, or have one or more projections known as 'ears'.

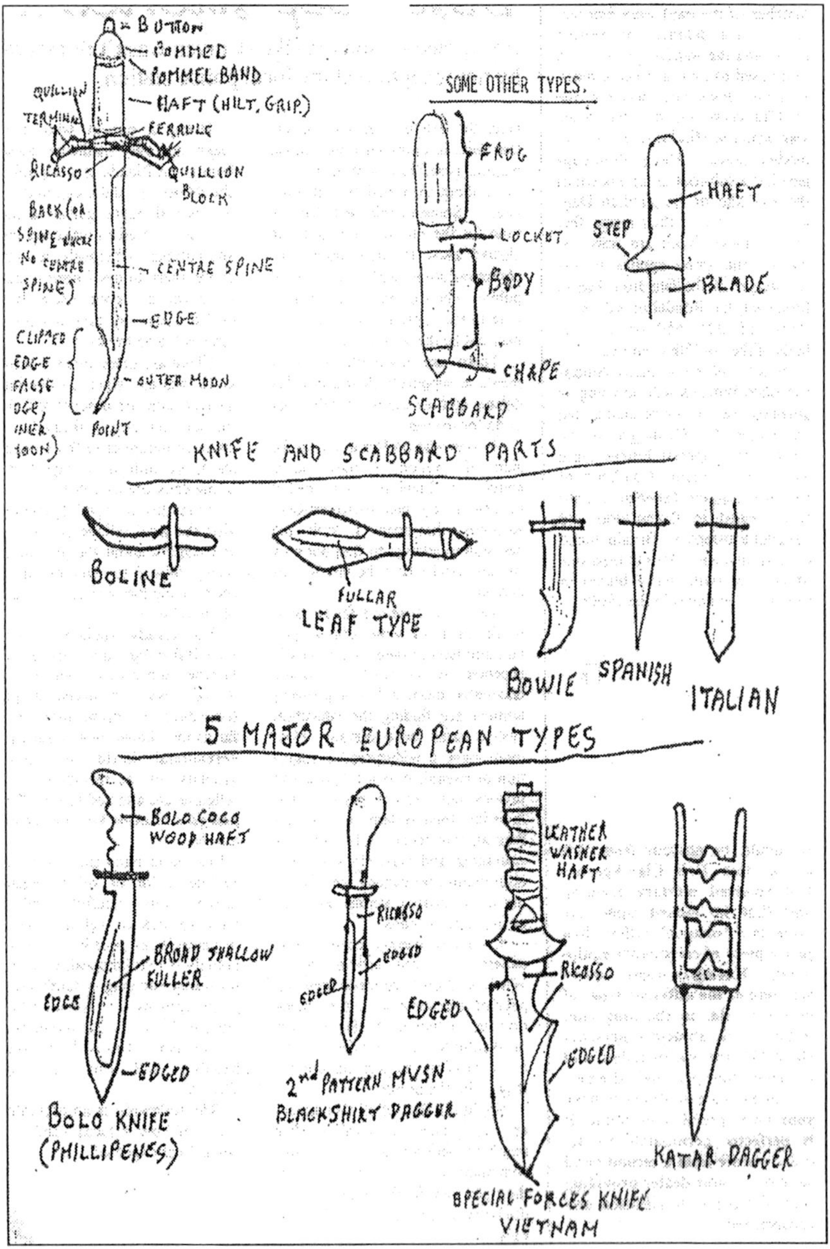
BUTTON
POMMEL
POMMEL BAND
HAFT (HILT, GRIP)
FERRULE
RICASSO
QUILLION BLOCK
BACK (OR SPINE WHERE NO CENTRE SPINE)
CENTRE SPINE
EDGE
CLIPPED EDGE
FALSE EDGE,
OUTER MOON
POINT
SOME OTHER TYPES.
FROG
LOCKET
BODY
CHAPE
SCABBARD
HAFT
STEP
BLADE
KNIFE AND SCABBARD PARTS
BOLINE
FULLAR
LEAF TYPE
BOWIE
SPANISH
ITALIAN
5 MAJOR EUROPEAN TYPES
BOLO COCO WOOD HAFT
BROAD SHALLOW FULLER
EDGE
EDGED
BOLO KNIFE (PHILLIPENES)
RICASSO
EDGED
2nd PATTERN MVSN BLACKSHIRT DAGGER
LEATHER WASHER HAFT
RICASSO
EDGED
EDGED
SPECIAL FORCES KNIFE VIETNAM
KATAR DAGGER

Inside the haft is the extension of the blade, either shaped or the same diameter as the blade, known as the 'tang'. This may be riveted in place to the haft. If the tang extends beyond the butt, it may be threaded and fastened by a screw known as a 'button'. If the butt is finished in a more elaborate way with a projecting part this, like the corresponding part of the sword, is called then 'pommel'. The pommel may also have a button and between the half and the bale there may be a metal ferrule.

Sometimes athames have a guard for the hand which is called by some, the 'hilt', while the handle is the haft or grip. The portion between the haft and the blade in this case, is known as the 'quillion block', while the extensions to either side are referred to as 'quillions'. The quillions may end in a ball or some other decoration which is called the 'terminal' (or terminals). Where there is no guard across the whole blade, the haft may have a single extension—on the blade edge side in the case of a single-edged athame. This is not a quillion, this is a step.

Blades may be of varying types and lengths but there are five main types of blade in Europe. You may say one shape for each point of the Pentacle. The parts, however, vary with the particular shape and design. Some blades have a portion immediately below the haft which is not sharpened to give added strength. This is known as the 'ricasso'.

The spine of the blade depends on its position with regard to the cross section of the blade. Where a small portion of the back of a blade is sharpened, this is known as a 'clipped edge' or 'false edge'. The blade may also have a groove running down most of its length called the 'blood trench' - a term often misunderstood by a soldier who has not been in service long. Called the trench or 'fuller', this is not to allow blood to flow out but to allow air to *get in* for ease of withdrawal — a point to note just in case you do sacrifice anyone!

The five main types of knife in use in European Covens can be classified as the boline, leaf, bowie, Spanish and Italian. The boline was developed from the *jambiya,* the type of dagger you see carried

---

All illustrations in this series are taken from Bob's original notes.

by the inhabitants of North Africa, with elaborately curved scabbards or sheaths. The blade is from 7 to 13 inches in the boline and 10½ to 13 inches in the *jambiya*. In the case of the *jambiya* and athames in the Balkan countries, the blade is frequently ribbed; that is, it has a raised spine down the centre of each side of the blade. This acts in the same way as the fuller.

The leaf blade is an ancient shape. It has been found in Stone Age knives and Bronze Age swords – and you can't get more traditional than that! The more modern type is similar in design to the Welsh *cledd* and I recognised one at a sabbat in 1947 as a Welsh machine gunner's knife used in trench warfare in 1916. I'm sorry to disappoint American folk-lore buffs but the bowie type, though perhaps used by Jim Bowie, is based on a North African design which has been in use at least as long ago as the Crusades.

Ridiculous as it may seem, the Spanish type is often seen in Italy, and usually referred to as the Mediterranean dirk. The blade narrows gradually and evenly from haft to point. The Italian pattern has a blade of equal width for most of its length before it suddenly narrows to a point.

Those are the five major athame types in Europe. In Scotland there are Witches who use the dirk as an athame. The Scots dirk evolved from the ballock knife. This form of knife being known to the Victorians as a 'kidney dagger' did not have quillions but instead had rounded prominences which may or may not account for its name. The major use in Europe was between 14th and 16th centuries. On the Baltic coats such a knife is known as a *poicke* and has a phaliform head with a conical pommel. The occult significance is obvious.

Confined also entirely to Italy, developing first in the north and later spreading to the south, were the knives known as *cinquedeas,* because just below the haft the blades was the width of five fingers. The blade length was 8 to 10 inches and they were in use between the 14th and 16th centuries. The blade was similar in shape to that of the *katar* knives used by the European gypsies.

Eared knives have been known since the Bronze Age but reached their peak of development in Spain, lasting in general use until at least 1380. Common knives used in the Middle Ages (and probably by Witches of the day) were *hauswehren* (home defence) or peasant knife, and the *weidprake,* or wood knife used to joint and carve meat. Properly developed between the 15th and 17th centuries, its time range was from the Middle Ages to early modern times. The quillion daggers have a sub-root group known as the Heraldic or Burgundian Dagger. Because of their rarity, few of the above types are now in use–the same applied to the *scramasax* of the late Iron Age to Medieval; the *rondel* or *scheibendoloch* of 1325-1550; or the *baselards* of the 14th to 15th centuries.

It is possible that many American male witches will be using as athames, war souvenirs such as the 2nd Pattern MVSN dagger, or the more recent Special Forces knife used in Vietnam. I do know of Fairburn daggers (Spanish stiletto type) issued to Commando and Parachute troops in Britain being used as athames. Also at least one Malay *kris* (with wavy blade) in use in the Midlands in the 1960s."

It should be obvious from the above that Bob Clay-Egerton had received an extensive military training and that he looked upon the knife as a weapon rather than just a piece of ceremonial equipment. This level of instruction was aimed at giving a clear understanding of the different types of knives and the magical symbolism represented by them. This would, in the long run, influence his student's choice in the construction and design of their own personal knife and the symbolism behind that choice.

There were those, of course, who dismissed all this information simply because they didn't see why they needed to learn about the different types of knife, or because they shied away from accepting the knife as anything other than a ritual tool. Bob's response was merely to point out that if they weren't willing to learn about the knife they wished to carry, then they weren't fit to carry one at all.

He was also adamant that it was perfectly permissible to acquire a second-hand athame provided that it was properly cleansed and consecrated. Bob and Mériém had a large collection of athames and swords which they used for ritual purposes and none of them were new, often being given as gifts by former associates.

The Chalice

The magical significance of the cup or chalice cannot be understated and that is why so much detail was given about the kind of design a Witch might be likely to choose ...

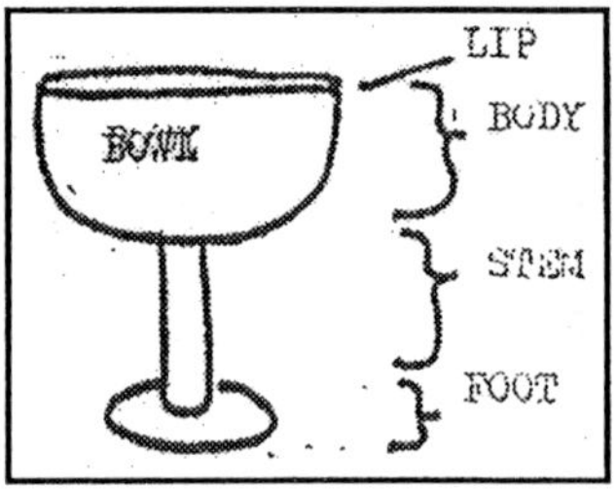

"Chalices used by Witches are of many and varied kinds – from a simple tea, or coffee cup, to elaborate antiques. They may be handle-less, or have one or more handles. They are of many materials ranging from wood to metal. Some stand on a paten, some do not; some have stems, some do not. Many are glasses normally used for drinking spirits or ale. Usually they comprise three parts: the bowl or body, the stem and the foot.

One thing they have in common at least, they must be given or presented, not bought by the Witch for his or her own use.

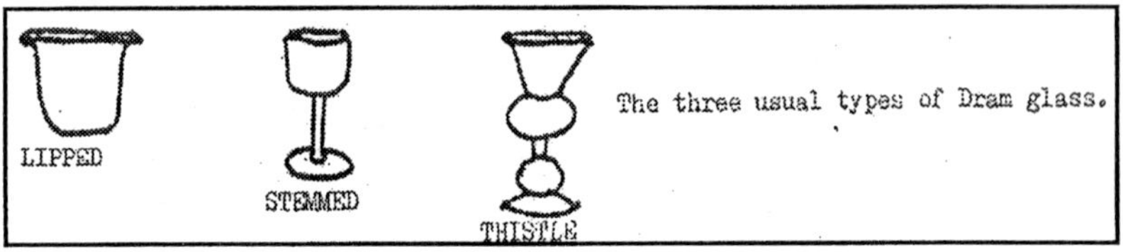

The three usual types of Dram glass.

Among the smaller chalices or cups are the Dram Glasses, popular since at least the 17th century. These are usually of three kinds. Rummers, popular in the late 18th century are larger and also of three kinds. Another kind of glass chalice is the type usually used in modern times to hold flowers, though they were introduced in the early 18th century as wine glasses. These are the long but narrow-bodied glasses known as Flutes.

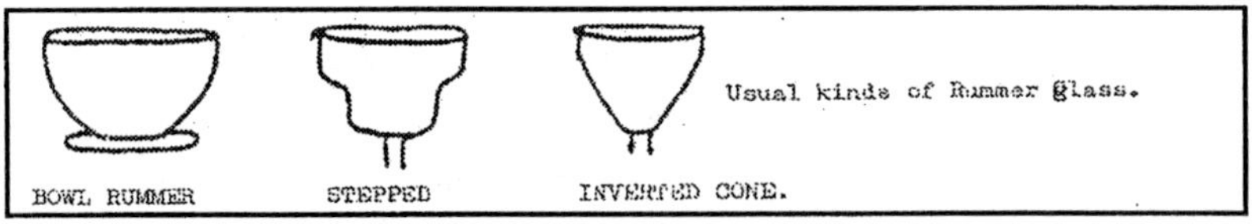

Usual kinds of Rummer Glass.

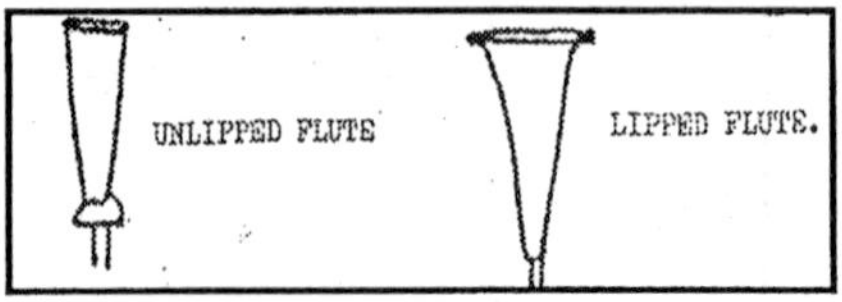

Feet or Legs: Occasionally chalices have legs, like a miniature cauldron; occasionally they stand in a special container like the Greek earthenware *matsos.* Some, like the Greek *skyphos* or *kotyle* bowls, have the body joined directly to a disk-foot, without a stem between. Some bowls, like the polygonal bowls, often of Japanese origin but developed from the Chinese Patiche vessels of the Chou Dynasty (1122-249BC) have neither stem nor foot, but nor does the lipped Dram Glass mentioned before.

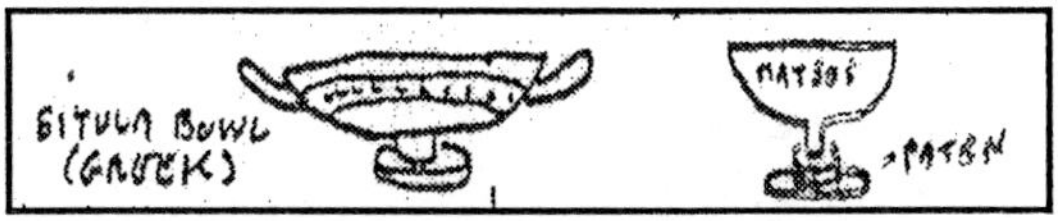

Bowls: Before a process of discolouration was invented in the 18th century, glass bowls were usually a dull green or blackish colour due to particles of iron in the silica. During the 17th century were four common shapes of glass bowl for glasses. These are known as the Straight Funnel, Round Funnel, the Waisted and the Bell Shaped. Greek bowls were of pottery and usually wide mouthed, the bowl being either shallow or deep and usually decorated inside, outside, or both. Few Greek bowls I think are used by British Witches, though I have known one in Warwickshire 20 years ago, and one in East Lancashire some six years ago.

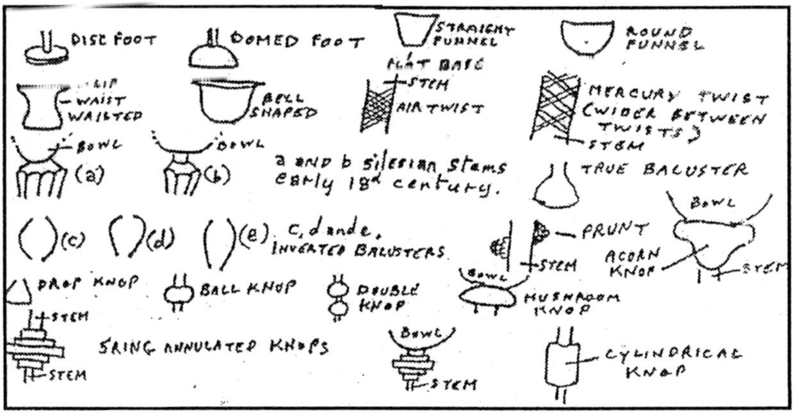

Stems and Knops: The stem is the part between the body and the foot of a chalice and it may be a straight piece of material, quite plain and cylindrical, or it may be fluted, spiralled, or have in it spirals of another material known as 'twists'. Also the stem may assume various shapes and these are known collectively as 'knops'. They include the Annulated knops with three, five, seven or nine rings or collars, Mushroom knops, Cylindrical, Acorn, Drop, Ball and Double knops. Similar to the knops are the Balusters, while on some stems of the more ornate kind, appear wart-like protuberances, often resembling raspberries, known as 'prunts'."

This article was Bob's way of demonstrating that you could use what the hell you liked as a chalice but that there were so many symbols to be found in the various different styles and types, that it paid to give a great deal of thought before choosing one for your own use, or offering one as a magical gift.

This attention to detail also gives a clue to just how poor his eyesight was at the time of writing that particular article. When finding such treasures at car boot sales, market stalls and antique shops, Bob would conduct a thorough examination with his fingers – and if the object 'spoke' to him then it would be carried home where it would undergo further scrutiny under his powerful magnifying glass.

The Pentacle

"The pentacle on your altar, that ancient symbol of protection used by Witches and magicians alike should be made of Earth materials, e.g. stone , slate, etc.

Its size, of course, depends on the size of your altar but I have known at least one altar where the pentacle was so large that it took up most of the space and almost took two men to lift it off. Personally, I think that was overdoing it a little. It is supposed to be a symbol of protection but if that one had fallen off the altar, the people in the flat below may have needed protection or compensation — but it would have made interesting reading on the insurance claim form.

Somewhere between 6 to 18 inches is a reasonable size and the thickness can vary. I think the majority of those in use in North Wales and Southern Cheshire are sheets of Welsh slate and so are some to be found in Cumbria and Westmorland.

The pentacle is in itself, a shield but when inscribed on material for use on an altar, the material on which the pentacle is inscribed becomes the shield proper–the inscription of the pentacle is the active-protective part of the shield.

The main part of the shield, whether circular, oval, square, rectangular or irregular (I have known a triangle and one that was carved in the shape of a pentacle from a solid piece of coal) has its obvious back, edges or edges, sides or corners where applicable. Upper and Lower Dexter on the right; Upper and Lower Sinister on the left and, no, not the front.

It is the Field that has the pentacle on it, while the pentacle itself is most appropriately called the Charge.

Although the usual pentacle used is called the five-pointed star and probably used by all Witches, I have known a Magician in Manchester who used the Shield of Daud, better known as the Star of David - though its name of the Shield of Daud gives away its esoteric importance. A Yememi Arab Magician of my acquaintance used instead the Sufic eight-pointed star.

With your five-pointed star you may, or may not, enclose it in a circle. You may, or may not, have an inner circle joining the points of the valleys. You may, or may not, have sigils or Hebrew characters between the arms or within the arms.

Only one more point. Don't forget to keep it clean–it will seem to attract dust after it has been charged."

In an historical context, the symbol of the five-pointed star can be found in the Pyramid Texts of ancient Egypt and so this really is the 'heraldic device' of the magical practitioner.

The Wand

"This section is devoted to wands or roads, not to staffs, staves or batons. The subject can be quite complex but as it is intended to familiarise the ordinary witch with the rod or wand, not to be an instruction manual for aspiring Staff Masters, I will have to be forgiven for perhaps not treating the subject with the detail with which it should be treated.

1. Parts of a Wand: These are as they apply to most designs – but not all. The Base, Butt, Heel, Foot or Hoof is at the extreme bottom end of the rod or wand. Foot or Hoof is the term especially used if the end *is* actually the foot or hoof of an animal, or part of one carved or moulded in the likeness of one.

2. Shank or Shaft: This is the main body of the wand.

3. Toe of the Rod: Occasionally called the head, this is the upper part of the rod where the diameter noticeably decreases to the tip. Except where the rod is:

a. of equal diameter top to bottom,
b. where the diameter decreases uniformly from top to bottom, like a snooker cue, or
c. where a separate toe is affixed, e.g. a crystal, needle, etc.,

4. Types of Base, Butt or Heel. The butt may be left completely flat where the rod has been cut across at right angles or a lesser angle. The flat section of the butt may be referred to as the Face. The butt may be carved or moulded into a shape, or have a butt of the same or different material affixed to it. Usual shapes are spherical, hemispherical, disc, pyramid (not usual and for explicit magical working). A fairly common butt in North Africa, also sometimes found in Spain and Southern France, is one in the form of the letter V or U - so that the rod looks like a miniature alpenstock. The shape denotes or symbolises horns, and in the Yemen is carried only by the leader of a group. If the butt is not of any particular shape, the end may have been carved or moulded into a

hollow, or the butt itself may be a hollow tube. In either case, the hollow is known as a Goblet and used to insert talismans, hair, water or other materials which are kept in by capping the butt with a plug.

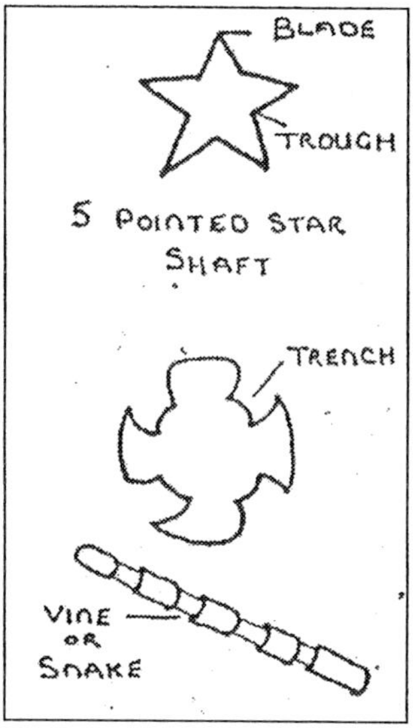

5. Shanks: If wood, these may be peeled or unpeeled, polished or unpolished, plain or signed. The shank is usually the same diameter from butt to toe—but not always. It may assume strange shapes such as a series of balls, but always straight (except for some specialised rods for specific magical purposes). Usually cylindrical and circular in cross section but it may, in cross section be square, triangular or hexagonal.

Unusual, but known, are wands whose cross section is that of a cross, or a 3, 5, 6 or 8 pointed star. Such shapes leave free standing arms of a cross or stars that are known as Blades. The gaps between the blades are called Troughs or Valleys. Where long, shallow cuts are made in the shaft and the cut is narrow (like a miniature canal), the cut is known as a Trench. A trench that spirals round the shank is referred to—in a wooden shanked wand—as a Vine, but if the wand is in non-wooden material, it is called a Snake.

A groove cut in a ring around the circumference of the shaft is known as a moat, but if the shaft is carved or moulded to leave a raised ring round the shaft this (or if there are more than one, these) are known as Collars, often with specific names.

A metal ring may be fitted around the shank, like a metal holding an eraser on the end of a pencil. This metal band is called a fillet (on the haft of an athame it would be called a tampion among other things). A fillet may be used to fit a butt or a toe to a shaft, but if it is not of metal, it is no longer a fillet, but a Binding.

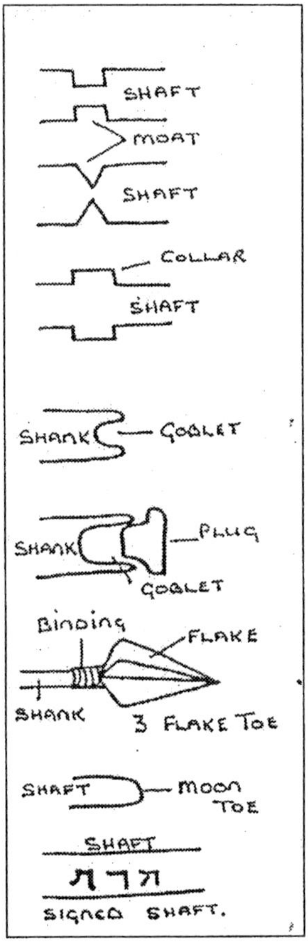

6. Toes: Like butts these can be of a different material to the shaft and of varying designs. They may have a goblet which will designate it as a 'toe goblet' as against a 'butt goblet'. For special magical purposes I have known a wand to have both. Crystals, often of quartz, may be fixed to the shaft as a toe, while other toes may be of bone, ivory, copper, steel, etc. They can be a needle or bodkin (self-explanatory), leaf shaped, or with jutting arms like the head of a hunting arrow where, instead of being called blades (as would be the case with an arrow), the up-standing pieces are known as Flakes.

A tapering end, like that of a sharpened pencil, is known as a Cone Toe. Like a butt, the toe may be completely flat with a face.; also like the butt, the face may be hemispherical. The centre of either of these faces, or the end of the toe furthest from the butt – the actual extremity of the toe – is known as the Point. A hemispherical toe face is called by some, a Moon Toe.

7. Signing: This is the decoration or individualising of the rod and may be done for pure decoration, or to have magical significance. The 'signature' may be moulded, carved, painted, engraved or embossed, on the shaft. It may consist of sigils, runes, symbols, floral decoration or gemstones, etc.

8. Materials: Wands may be made of almost any material. Glass, metal, wood, ebony, ivory bone – I have even known the alloy arrow from a steel bow used.

9. Size: Wands may range from an inch or so (not usual) to the distance between the end of the middle finger to the elbow. The end of finger to shoulder, or between elbow and shoulder, is a Baton and above this comes the Major Baton, the Staffs and the Staves."

Like the knife, the wand is a very personal magical item and should be treated as such, especially if it is one no longer in use. Should it be necessary to dispose of a wooden wand, then an ideal solution is to return to the mother tree (or one of the same species) from which the wand was cut and bury it deep down among the root system.

The Cross

"It is easy, when discussing crosses, to become involved in deep esoteric meanings involving the elements, the cardinal points, the interfaces, the Sufic eight pointed cross, the Abyssal inter-dimensions between the arms of the crosses or their points, etc. I am just going to give a few items of information which you may already know.

The cross was used by the worshippers of Baal, not to inflict a contemptible death but an *honourable* one. Only the best, human or animal, were subjected to crucifixion as a sacrifice to Baal. A Carthagian general seeking victory, is reported as having dressed his son in the finest clothes before sacrificing him on a cross.

The cross was a symbol of *Faith* and that is the reason illiterate people, when asked to "Make their mark" as a signature, made a cross, trusting that this would prevent their 'signature' being used for an evil purpose. The Greek Cross, with arms of equal length, has even found its way into the Royal Regalia of Britain and may be seen on some crowns and surmounting the orb.

The Tau Cross, shaped like the Greek letter T with a vertical leg and a cross bar on top, was an early symbol of authority and carried like a sceptre or a field marshal's baton. Greek bishops carry a crosier which is in the form of a Tau Cross; the modern version of this symbol of authority can be seen in the Chairman's gavel. To the ancient Egyptians, the Tau Cross was the symbol of Thoth, the God of Wisdom and Healing. The sacred monogram of Thoth is a Tau Cross either in a circle, or surmounting a circle. This is a symbol of the God of Wisdom protecting the world and later became a symbol for the Earth. As a sigil on a talisman it was used to protect from hidden dangers.

In the East, talismans resembling Tau Crosses - and known as Crutches – are common. They are formed by an elongated letter or group of letters making up a word. This is usually the name of a prophet, saint, or an attribute of God. In addition to the above are the Swastika, a cross with bent arms, and the Wheeled Cross.

The Swastika is well known in both hemispheres. In Scandinavia and Northern Europe it was known as the Hammer of Thor, who equates with the Egyptian Horus. In a war with the Giants, Thor threw his hammer (and I can assure you that a fighting hammer is not a weapon to be scorned in the hands of an expert), and the weapon turned four times in flight, this being symbolised by the four legs of the cross. The hammer, like the boomerang, always returned after being thrown though unlike the Aboriginal weapon it came back after striking the target.

The Swastika was also the symbol of the Sun to some pagans and is shown on the Bayeaux Tapestry in conjunction with the Christian Cross, signifying that William considered himself the Witch King of England by right, as well as being nominally a Christian in order to get the Pope's blessing for the invasion. As the founder of my line; Egerton of Egerton and Oulton, was William's sister's son I suppose that I may be a traditional Witch. (Just as well, since I don't think Alex [Sanders] would have had me.)

In medieval churches, north of a line from the Humber to the Dee (the old Northumbria), bells often had the Swastika Cross marked on them, to give the still-pagans-at-heart, reassurance that the Christian Church they had to use was properly protected. In the islands of the South Seas, China, Japan and India the Swastika is a sign of long life and happiness. One presumes that they have not been hit by a flying hammer.

The symbol of a four armed cross became a sigil meaning Earth (like that of Thoth), and sometimes there were several crosses forming the spokes of a wheel. To the Druids the centre, where the crosses' radiating arms passed, symbolised the Sun. The radiating arms, or spokes, symbolised the planets and the outer circle was the symbol of infinity and eternity. The symbol is also used to denote the Sun and as such is used as a protective talisman being seen as the highest placed of the brasses on a horses' harness to protect horse and rider, or cart. It was used on military shields, and on coins, such as those of Edward the Elder 901-925 A.D. In the Derbyshire village of Bradwell there are moulded cartwheels on the ceiling of a café; while houses used to have wheel symbols built into the walls as a protection against fire.

The wheel of the Law is one of the Buddha's Great Glorious Emblems and people in the East turn Wheel Crosses to bring about a change of luck, bringing good luck up and letting bad luck fall away as the wheel swings. In Tibet the wheels are used to help prayers ascend to the Gods.

In the times of the Witch hunts they were not so fortunate. Many Witches were 'broken on the wheel', so it could be said that they were sacrificed also, on the Wheeled Cross rather than that of Baal."

The Dance

"According to some medieval and later sources, evil Witches danced Widdershins in a circle (or anti-clockwise), against the path of the Sun. To dance Sun-wise is to dance Deosil and so modern Witches dance Deosil so that they can claim not to be evil since they follow the path of the Sun. Unfortunately, it has been reasonably well proven that the Sun does *not* revolve around the Earth and neither does it have a noticeable path. The apparent path is caused by the Earth turning on its axis in its own Path around the Sun.

The Sun appears to travel from left to right, East to West, that is Deosil. *To create this effect the Earth turns Widdershins!* So the Witches allegedly devoted to the Goddess (represented by the feminine Moon, not the masculine Sun) and to the Goddess of the Earth, nowadays dance in *opposition* to the path of the Earth and in the apparent direction of the masculine Sun. The Witches who pay a little more than lip-service to their faith, and are prepared to take it further than an adult play-group session (a minority, I rather fear), will state that they dance the Moon Path and not the Sun path.

A spinning, or turning body, like a planet, by its own motion creates a magnetic gravitational field that seems to be dependent for measurable strength on the size of the body and its rate of rotation. It has been demonstrated that a group of people dancing in a circle produces a definite energy flow similar to that of an electric field. This is apparently enhanced when the circle is of alternate males and females, especially when they are holding hands (i.e. in contact with each other).

It may be that the direction danced, either Deosil or Widdershins, affects the field in some way. We do not know. Insufficient work has been done on the subject but knowledge does not come freely on a platter. So, evoke the Lord of the Dance, and take the steps necessary to improve yourself spiritually."

An Introduction to Occultism

This was the title of one of Frater Asmodaeus's tapes, many of which are still in circulation, although the quality often leaves a lot to be desired. A surviving recording was recently described as sounding as though he'd recited it in a wind-tunnel. The following was taken from Bob's original hand-written notes:

"Various fallacies are current in the occult world which separate the men from the boys; the inexperienced or the unknowledgeable from those who have at least attained basic knowledge. Surprisingly, many occult authors, whose work in their own field may be generally good, seem to be unaware of making basic mistakes.

To some extent, this is part of the emperor's-suit-of-clothes syndrome. In the fairy story, the con-man tailor said that only an idiot would be unable to see (and presumably feel) the clothes he was making for the king. As a result, king, queen, courtiers and the general populace pretended to admire the non-existent suit of clothes worn by the naked king (It can be assumed the tailor also made his under garments.) No one wished to admit to being totally stupid. Only one small boy, who hadn't heard of the king's magic clothes, spoke up and punctured the bubble of self-deceit.

Frater Asmodaeus behaves as did that small boy. He will puncture the bubble of falsehood, no matter how eminent the author or speaker, for in occult matters it is truth that matters. False notions are like the emperor's magic clothes. Many such falsehoods are perpetuated by hundreds of years of hearsay and tradition. As a result, they become implanted in the collective subconscious; they encourage and support further falsehoods.

For example. For hundreds of years, Witches were (in fact, still are) supposed to be evil, doing harm to both animals and man and worshipping a man-hating devil. Many of us know that this is not true—some Witches do good!

Frater Asmodaeus does evil because he is no respecter of persons. He casts doubt on the old beliefs that Witches are evil. He tells the truth as he sees it, even if it gets up a person's nose. *But on* what authority does he do this? Answer: On his own authority as an individual! Not as a High Priest; as a 9th Degree of the Treble O; as a Warden of Alderley Edge, or as any other high-faluting, classy-sounding title or ego-boosting position in any occult group. On his own individual study and questioning during over 50 years in the occult—as more of an arse-kicker than an arse-licker.

What he has to say in his talks, articles and tapes is likely to be controversial. If you want a placid, easy-going, everything handed to you on a plate existence—then have nothing to do with him. Banish him! Exorcise him! For he may make you *think* and ruin your complacency forever.

It is said in the holy Qur'-án of the Muslim, "Your religion is not made hard for you." People like Asmodaeus make *anyone's* religion hard. He makes you work to understand it, sweat and suffer to progress. But on the way, you may find that, in truth, the labourer is worthy of his hire.

If you accept that hundreds of years of brain-washing from childhood about the Earth being flat; or the Sun and Planets revolving around the earth; or the Earth being the centre of the Universe, and the evil of Witches and their ways, are falsehoods. Even though, in their day these were 'facts', believed and upheld by the most knowledgeable men of their time. If you accept these as falsehoods then you must be prepared to go further and realise that the progression of falsehood did not cease suddenly in the 18th century–it goes on today.

Are you ready to be 'born again' to begin, in time, to see a far off glimpse of the 'kingdom of god'? To be 'born again' you must as Christ said, "Become as a little child". You must totally reject all teachings from babyhood and start again with only your *original* instincts–not even those developed later as you grew up and taught to you by others.

Read and listen, *think, think*! Without being prejudiced by earlier teachings. This will not be easy at first. But *think! Think! Think* again!

When a person first encounters the occult world it is usually through stories or books, first read to them as a child, then read by them once they've learned to read. These are fairy tales but what do they instil in the mind of a child? That all step-mothers are evil. That all giants are bad.

Is there a single fairy story in which there is a 'good' step-mother? Is it any wonder that so many step-children are pre-conditioned to resent a step-mother or step-father in European countries? The Oedipus complex may be the answer of the psychiatrist even if this only applies to boys. What about a Brothers Grimm complex?

They may have a lot to answer for, because how many jolly Green Giants do you read about in children's books? In *Jack & the Beanstalk* the giant was a cannibal who ate Englishmen. What was wrong with the flesh of a Scot, a Welshman, Irishman or

Channel Islander? Such stories cause a deep dislike of giants, green or otherwise. At the same time, they teach that it is quite alright to trespass on private property, enter someone's home, steal his money and, if he chases you, to cause his death—as long as he is a giant, someone different or unusual. Do this and you will live happily ever after.

Of course, you may hear or read of a 'good' fairy-godmother, who works supposedly 'good' magic for *Cinderella* (possessed of a wicked stepmother and two ugly sisters). In reality, the 'fairy god-mother' is a con-artist. By her magic she cons the door-keeper at the ballroom, the prince and the genuine guests. Was her magic 'good'? It was not done for self, so it could be answered, yes.

But what of the mice transformed into horses and coachmen? At midnight they became mice again. Miles from a place they know and any young they may have; prey to owls, badgers, foxes, etc., and in strange surroundings. Is this good magic? As good as the fairy stories that are still believed and promulgated by many occultists ...

"One of the most proliferate occult fairy stories is that of black and white magic. Black magic is supposed to be evil and white magic, good. Black magic is supposed to be the 'black art' - but what is the *original* 'black art'? It is alchemy! Its very name pro-claims it – and I *am* being serious; not in my usual bantering, leg-pulling mood. The ancient name for the land of Egypt was Khem, spelt in English K.H.E.M – when the annual flooding of the Nile was over and the waters receded, they left behind huge quantities of *black*, fertile mud. Khem means 'the black land'.

Egypt was one of the homes of magic (as was Sumeria) and this black land was 'Al Khem' from which came 'alchemy' - the art of the black land. When magic was condemned by the church it was easy to ascribe to the theory that magical knowledge was black and evil, the opposite of miracles, which were white and good.

I have heard 'black' magic defined as magic which is done for personal gain, while white magic is done for the good of others. Why do good for others? I am told that by doing so, you grow spiritually—and apart from that, you feel better for having done so.

If you grow spiritually as a result of these actions (or even feel better because of them), *you* are gaining from your actions and so by qualification they *must* be black.

All hail to the hypocrites!

Also, how do you know that what you do really is for the good of others? For example: a woman is ill and unable to leave the hospital for a month. You are a supposedly 'white' witch or magician, so you do a little white healing magic and she recovers in three weeks. Feeling much better by the fourth week she goes shopping, is hit by a car driven by a joy-rider and spends the rest of her life – 50 or 60 years – paralysed from the neck down. If you'd not interfered with your 'white' magic, she'd have been safe in hospital, a damn sight less ill and able to recover.

For once and for all, there is no such thing as black and white magic, or black and white witchcraft. The actions, good or bad, are solely the province of the individual. What matters is the sincerity of intention, not the act itself.

I would even go so far as to say that what may seem good to one generation, may appear evil to another. At one time it was 'good and godly' to torture, hang and burn Witches – now it is evil. The churches, both Catholic and Protestant, that committed these atrocities still, in the main, see witches as evil. Are they then good christians – because many Witches and magicians still follow this system of brain-washing and refer to magic as black or white. All are judging, yet Christ said: "Judge not lest ye be judged", while the Wiccan Rede is: "An it harm none—do as ye will".

Whatever they may say, Christian and Witch alike, judge others and harm their reputations. All are adversaries and opponents of both others and each other. Now according to ancient Hebrew, an adversary or opponent is a *satan* – because that's what the word means. To my way of thinking, most (if not all) christians and most (if not all) Witches are, in the true sense of the word, Satanists! And I prefer the true sense of a word to a false, manufactured one.

The experienced occultist is driven to using all this double talk as a result of a mistake made by an eminent occultist, and preached and published in sincerity. I refer, of course, to the ridiculous reversion of the 'left and right hand paths'. Before the mistake was compounded by the great Madame Blavatsky, the Jews, poaching their ideas from the older civilisations of Philistia, Sumeria and Egypt (among others) knew that the harsh light of the Sun, i.e. the day, during which the right arm fought and toiled. So the day and the right hand were considered to be male. The softer light of the Moon, and the night, when one could rest and sleep, was attributed to the female. The night, being opposite to the male, was the left hand.

Madame Blavatsky was an east-European lady, of good family, with at least the upper middle-class social mores of the day when a woman was the property of her husband and sex was a duty not to be enjoyed by any respectable lady. Madame B. was a true product of her time and upbringing. She married but it seems she may well have been frigid.

She visited India and, being accepted as a genuine occultists, was permitted to attend a ceremony of one of the cults of the Varma Marg–from the Sanskrit meaning 'left hand path'. There she witnessed a young woman among many men, apparently being 'used' by an old man for the purpose of his oral sexual gratification. Apparently not having a clue what was going on (and incidentally there is no *actual* physical contact between the priest and priestess, though this would not be apparent to an onlooker), Madame Balvatsky's European morals were offended. Henceforth she wrote and spoke extensively of the horrific 'evil' of the left hand path, referring to what she saw as 'black magic'.

So, today, we have Witches venerating a female goddess of the moon, calling themselves followers of the masculine, solar, right hand path, and decrying the left hand path (which they don't realise they follow), as evil.

As a result, the experienced occultist now has the compounded problem–purely for the sake of communication, you understand–to use double talk and say 'left' when he means 'right' and 'right' when he means 'left'!

Conventional Morality

Whenever serious occultists get together, sooner or later, the question of morality will enter the discussion. The Laws of Magic, if followed correctly are extremely moral. This does not mean the laying down of rules and regulations, it merely means that the Witch or magician is totally responsible for their own actions both within and without the magic circle.

"For example, magically speaking there are different reasons, basically concerned with personal energy patterns and flows, that may (should the occasion arise) require a man or woman to work with another person who is not their partner. Needless to say, such statements often result from Ophidian uninitiated and those still subconsciously in thrall to their early training, in recriminations.

These range from accusations of male chauvinism, through being a lecherous old (or young) man, to protestations that such activities should be carried out only by partners 'in love' with each other. Of such accusations, I prefer the first two, though neither really applies in Ophidian magic if embarked on with sincerity.

As for love, I have found that, of those who most proclaim love for their fellow men, not a few are consummate rip-off artists and feeders on the thoughts and words of others. Perfect love is one of the two 'perfect' words used by modern Witches. Perfect bitch-craft might well be another. Love, in the occult sense has more than one meaning, of course, and is not confined within the boundaries of conventional morality."

The Power of Evil

This article was dated 28th February 1994; nearly a decade before the events of 11th September 2001, which shows how little things have changed ...

"A gentleman of my acquaintance always seems to be upset when he sees me. Upon sighting me he usually proceeds to speak loudly of the iniquity of witchcraft and the power of evil in the world. It does seem that he is correct in assuming that there is a power of evil in the land, though I would not attribute it to witch-craft. This despite my knowledge and experience of the practices of some who call themselves followers of the Craft.

Where does evil obtain its great power? My acquaintance would have us believe that it is from the followers of Satan, Witches, magicians, Tarot readers, astrologers, all branches of the occult and anyone who does not agree with the particular branch of fundamentalist christianity to which he subscribes. I do not agree completely, though I must accept that many occultists (including myself), assist in giving strength to evil.

There are intentional supporters of evil out there, it is true, but the support and strength that they give evil is negligible. By far the greatest degree of strength and support that evil receives comes from all of us who, while not seeming to support it, do so *by failing to oppose it!* A fine statement, but if we are to oppose it, how do we know what is evil?

Evil, like good, is relative. That which constitutes good, whole-some, socially acceptable and applaudable behaviour in one society, is often regarded by another as uncouth, reprehensible, utterly unacceptable and evil. As a result, it may come about that one person, or group of people, in opposing strongly what *they* deem to be evil are, in fact, supporting, strengthening and encouraging it. A case of: "But of good cometh forth evil."

Does this sound impossible? Look back in history. The early Christian church had a disagreement and a vote was taken at a council of church leaders to decide the matter. One side won by barely fifty per cent of the vote. In a very short time and using the authorisation of having won, the followers of the winning clique had commenced the extermination of those who favoured the loosing argument. In other words, change your beliefs, in the name of Christ, or be put to the sword by your fellow christians.

Later they started work on other factions whom they suspected of disagreeing with them. Now they tortured for 'confessions' before hanging or burning those considered to be not only *their* opponents but the enemies of God. Not only humans were tortured and murdered, animals also suffered in great numbers—but these torturers and murderers claimed to be opposing evil.

Today, what do we find in this modern, high-tech, 20th century society? We find Islamic, Hindu, Jewish and christian fundamentalists all fighting evil. The Hindus destroying mosques to build temples; the Muslims putting death sentences on authors and killing numbers of clerics who refuse to toe a hard and questionable line. Jewish fundamentalists murdered Arabs, even those who were friendly: men, women and children.

They hanged British soldiers and blew up men, women and children in the King David's Hotel in Jerusalem. Two of their terrorist leaders became Prime Ministers when they gained their own 'homeland'. A homeland? The Ashkanazi incomers from Eastern and Western Europe and the Americas dispossessed those Chesidic Jews who had lived for centuries in Palestine. These had few rights compared to the incomers who took over the government. All in the name of good.

What of the christian fundamentalists? They help to give us bogus child sexual-abuse scandals, aimed at destroying paganism. They picket New Age shops but are never accused of fire bomb attacks on such places, or malicious damage. They are all doing 'God's' work. Let them gain power and we may well see the fires burning again – or the modern equivalent.

Each of us has to decide for ourselves what is good and what is evil. Not all is good in the pagan world. Make a joke or write an article knocking Odin and you will soon know about it as some of the Northern Tradition followers go berserk! It is the same with other traditions. All see evil where none is intended, and while expending their energies on opposing what they deem attacks on their path, it may be that they fail to oppose true evil; helping it to gain strength and power, by falling out amongst themselves.

and Media Junkies

Once again, at Samhain, we have been treated to the annual attack on the occult by the fanatical fringe of those impostors who call themselves christians, assisted by their minions of the media. The usual 'unbiased' television presentation with its now predictable line-up of selected occultists (almost always Gardnerian Wiccans), versus selected christians. One of these unbiased programmes commenced with three grotesquely made-up women, cackling out the lines of the three Witches from Shakespeare's *Macbeth.* A good 'unbiased' start to what was supposed to be a serious programme.

Predictably, the side of sweetness and light had along their tame psychiatrist, their ex-Witch (who again had a remarkable dearth of knowledge about the religion she was supposed to have been a member of, talking of free drugs, drinking blood and other horrors too terrible to mention). How convenient! It ended, as expected, with a representative of the christian side having the last word on the subject.

Historically one thing *has* changed. Although all occultists, including witches, are *still* termed followers of the Devil, almost imperceivably, our christian brethren have ceased to refer to Hindus, Muslims and Buddhists in the same way. The fact, of course, that countries where these religions are paramount are now politically important, has nothing to do with this modern prevailing attitude.

The Church Militant has, in this respect at least, been forced to relinquish its following of the Way of Peace, by waging bloody war. The followers of such religions, were not all prepared to continue to turn the other cheek. They fought when need be, in many ways, to retain the right to follow their religion.

What we see today from the supporters of occultism *per se*, is all too frequently a weak, almost pleading attempt to justify the various branches of paganism. And all too frequently, we see one group of pagans standing aloof from other paths and making it plain that *they* are different. This attitude the Church Militant loves and fosters. Those occult apologists, gently waving the white flag, trying to use honest answers (which sound more like attempts to plead that their own path is unique and closer to christianity), do no real good against the power of the entrenched church.

They are not fighting kind gentlemen who courteously adhere

to an elegant set of rules of fair play. They face a wolf in sheep's clothing. A master of fair words who is only prepared to withhold violence, as long as the social code and the law states that this must be so. Let the repeal of the Witchcraft Act be annulled and the Church Militant will erupt again, as it has done in the past. This enemy has *all* the advantages. Wealth, power, control of the media in all its forms, control of education so that children are brainwashed almost from birth against anything to do with occultism and especially against the 'wicked Witch'.

Let those who will continue to fight the good fight, answering questions, always on the defensive, showing how good and pure occultists really are. For all my criticism they believe they are doing a good job–and so they are. But surely there are those who think along the same lines as me: that enough is enough. The time has come to make a stand; not only to make a stand but to fight back.

Let us cease to meekly answer questions on radio and TV, giving truthful, though mealy-mouthed, answers. Let *US* start asking the questions! Yes *US!* Let them be as awkward to answer as we wish to make them. Let us ask why for hundreds of years, a church of the Prince of Peace has condoned not only the torture and murder of 'pagans', but even those christians whose beliefs differed little from theirs? Why the churches preach that you cannot worship both God and Mammon, yet they themselves, as institutions, hold so much wealth? Why the churches are so intolerant of those whose religions do not number millions? Why their Holy Books are so full of contradictions, errors and blatant untruths? Why they are afraid to let their opponents have an equal opportunity to put their case openly on television in the way that speakers representing other faiths and other branches of christianity, may?

We know why they fear, but the brainwashed public does not, and it is that audience we need to convince. Too many of the 'committed' christians should be exactly that–committed, if not for mental disturbance due to fanaticism, but for criminal damage, stirring up public disorder and assault against occultists who are supposed, under the UN Charter of Human Rights, to be free to worship as they wish.

Time Wasting

Despite his fighting talk, Bob was always ready to meet and debate with representatives from any religion. When a Chinese friend suggested he go along to a local inter-faith 'drop-in' that catered for people of all denominations, he willingly agreed to the visit ....

"About 3.00pm a group of people arrived, mostly male who cheerily said "hello" and took immediate possession of a large table, encircling it completely. They at once commenced to talk avidly amongst themselves, ignoring everyone except the lady in charge of the centre, who was kept busy (despite walking with a pronounced limp), in supplying the group with refreshments. If they had come to meet and speak with the clients, they showed little inclination to do so. We felt that our presence was something of an embarrassment.

By 3.25pm, most of the clientele had followed the proverbial example of the Bedouin and had 'silently packed their tents and left'. That left one lady, two gentlemen (my Chinese friend had already left) and myself at one table; a somewhat embarrassed lady behind the counter with a volunteer worker; and the same eight religious ladies and gentlemen still in animated discussion around the commandeered table.

It was 3.35pm when we outcasts decided to leave – the first time I think that anyone had stayed beyond closing time. As we arose, the door opened to admit the Bishop and the Methodist leader. It is ungracious of me to think, even for a moment, that they had deliberately waited until the centre had officially closed for the day in order not to have to meet the *hoi-polloi*, the lower orders and those not engaged in Holy Orders. They may have heard that I was to be there – an occultists and member of several unholy Magical Orders in my time.

As I left the room, I turned and said loudly, "I thank you, first for the invitation to meet you all. Secondly, for your delightful company, and thirdly for your views, so eloquently expressed in our enlightening conversation. I now commence to perceive, as may those who were here earlier to meet you, what was meant by Christ when He said 'Inasmuch as ye do this unto the least of these my brothers--ye do it unto me!' I then smiled, raised my right hand in blessing with the sign of the Horns and wished them: 'Blessed Be!'"

Perhaps I was wrong to speak thus but at least two of us had changed our plans, perhaps to the inconvenience of others. In my case, maybe to the discomfort of someone who had genuinely needed my advice or help. The lady in charge of the centre had gone out of her way to persuade us to attend to meet these dignitaries. She had been paid by embarrassment and, in my friend's case, 'loss of face'. Why? Though some of the customers were obviously poor and badly clothed, my friend and a couple of the others were well dressed.

They did not need to fear that an alms bowl might have been presented, or a request made for charity. It was as if no one outside their group existed. I have, on occasions, experienced and myself used, the Cloak of Invisibility but with no occult group have I experienced such a brilliantly executed negative use of the Cloak. An instance where it is not the subject that is invisible to the observers, but the observers being invisible to the subject!

There must be a lesson here that the Goddess is seeking to impress upon me. It could be: 'Cast not your pearls before swine, lest they trample them underfoot'. Or it could be: 'Be not diverted from the path once chosen'. It is unfortunate that, my time on this Earth being limited, I have to have it wasted by such people. It makes me consider that, as my time was wasted by these purveyors of religion, so must I be careful that I do not waste the time of others by arranging to meet them, and then making a mockery of the meeting.

For in taking such action we harm ourselves. Further it may be that we do only offend those who may not be in a position to address the balance against us, we may offend One who can. By wasting time, we may offend the Goddess of Periodic Time who, as Kali, is also a destroyer. She might well destroy some of our Time, or set to nought by destroying that which we have lovingly spent so much time in building or achieving."

17th March 1994

Middle Working

Never wishing to miss an opportunity to explain the ways of the Wise, conventional morality was the subject of a rather unexpected talk that Bob was asked to give under the most bizarre of circumstances.

"In the 1960s, in Warwickshire, the christian fundamentalists were not so well organised as they are now, 30 years later. One smallish group regularly hired a meeting place in our local town, where there were six covens within a 12 mile radius, all associated with the parent coven, the Moonrakers.

Soon after they became active, the pastor of the evangelical group was overheard by one of the witches, talking about the expenses incurred in getting preachers to visit from outside the area. Now Witches are supposed to be malicious, so this Witch interrupted, excused himself and said that he knew of someone living in the area who was accustomed to preaching and who did not charge for furthering 'the word'.

Being a twittle-head, the pastor was grateful to be given my name and address—or at least the name I would be using—and wrote asking if I would be prepared to give a sermon or a lesson, free or for expenses only. I agreed to speak at no charge, and had his letter photocopied, remembering the first Law of the Occult—"Trust none!"

On the appointed Sunday I turned up, in a suit, no less! So did a number of members of the Moonrakers and the hived-off covens. The story is, from memory, the sermon I gave before the riot started ... [This lengthy tirade was couched in Bible-thumping style in the best traditions of Frater Asmodaeus and far too long and tedious to be included here ...]

It was around this stage that shouts of "Author! Author!", "Well said, sir!" and "That's telling the buggers!" arose and the first punches were thrown by the x'tian militants—rather naturally since witches are usually peaceful people, fanatics are not.

When the storm had sped, as it says in *Forever Amber*, we made our way home, to be later visited by the police who had been told that I was the cause of the disturbance. I produced a photocopy of the pastor's letter requesting that I give a free talk, and suggested they charge him with action liable to cause a breach of the peace, or for wasting police time. They withdrew and we saw them in the village no more–until the commencing of the Warwickshire Witch-hunts a few months later.

Points of View

This piece first appeared in *Phoenix* magazine. "Once again the spoon of discord is dipped into the occult cauldron of faeces and given a deft twist. The resultant spray hits the fan of distribution and no one is safe.

This time the shower is directed towards [occult] advertisers and also towards 'names'. Advertising comes, like the advertisers, in many shapes and sizes. Often advertisements are reasonably accurate in their description of goods and/or services. Too frequently, they are not.

May I, who do not normally foretell the future make a prediction? It will be the first thing I've been able to make this year, even the four and twenty novices who came down from Inverness, escaped unsullied.

We have in this country all manner of High Priestesses, High Priests, Magisters, Sadhus, Mullahsw, Teachers and even Guru Witches. Some are genuine, some are always serious. Some, like Crowley, Sanders and others play the fool to the general public, and thereby attract from the serious students only those with sufficient insight to pierce the disguise and camouflage. We have, of course, also the genuine bloody idiot and the apparent idiot who is able to rook the gullible.

So, if I may make my prediction.

It is that many newcomers to the occult will answer advertisements in occult, or pseudo-occult magazines, find they are being ripped off and turn against any further exploration. No matter that negative *karma* will be stored up against the advertiser, or that the would-be student should not have been so easily discouraged, it is the general image and reputation of the occult *per se* – our name and a reputation, that suffers.

Bitchcraft is bad enough, but this false posturing by High Priests and High Priestesses of Mammon, Profits and Profitesses of the fast buck, should not be tolerated. There are several magazines that carry advertisements making claims to a long history and offering courses of instruction in witchcraft. To teach well, you have to know your subject intimately. A teacher is a guru. Can one have a Guru-Witch or a Tantric-Wiccan, or even an Egyptian Wiccan? One might, but will their claims stand close investigation?

How many unsuspecting novices have expended their hard-earned £10 and received in return four pages of questionable information? It has been written that 'The labourer is worthy of his hire'. To my view, these so-called teachers haven't laboured hard but are on double-time, plus bonus, regardless. Things get worse! You can get Initiation, but at a price! For my £40 I'd want initiation into the Tantric rites of a superior cat-house and a season ticket into the bargain. The course is run by a Witch Queen!

It's no good writing to the magazine in question to complain. They won't print your letter. Not against such a large, regular, fee-paying advertiser. The magazine is in the business to make a profit, not to ensure that divertisements are genuinely able to give satisfaction. If you don't like it and want to complain, be careful how you do it.

Take the obvious statements –ask if the advertiser can *prove* the alleged age of their particular path; their coronation and public acclaim as Queen/King by other Witches; who will stand guarantor for them? Ask this of the Advertising Standards Board – let them take action."

Demonic Agitation

Five decades of occult study and practice have perchance taught me one or two things. One thing which I have learned is that the supernatural powers have a sense of humour. Also I have learned that some of the adherents of occult paths, or branches of occult paths, have not yet ascertained this fact.

It states in the Holy Qur'-án that: "Your religion is not made hard for you". It is written in Bukhari Hadith that the Prophet Muhammad was invited to a wedding and that, on arriving at the venue, found everyone deadly serious. The Prophet asked: "Where are those who beat the *duff*?" (a small drum. It is normal to have dancing, even if segregated, and merriment at an Arab wedding.

Because the Prophet had been invited, some ostentatious knuckle-head had assumed and persuaded the others that drum beating, dancing and merriment would be unseemly in the holy man's presence. Unfortunately such knuckle-heads are not confined to the followers of Islam, not even to some sects of Judaism, nor christianity, though the deities know that enough abound there.

They are to be seen and heard like the saints who come marching in, in their numbers in the ranks of occultists. It would seem that they have barely moistened their lips in Parnassus, and that of the Well below Ygdrassil they have heard only a Murmyr. Not only do they hedge themselves around with iron-bound ritual but they believe that the old gods cannot laugh at themselves. They are still subconsciously affected by such sentiments, learned in christian childhood as "Thou shalt not take the name of the Lord thy God in vain."

Have they learned nothing of 'intention' and have they forgotten, or choose to ignore, "God knows that which is in thy heart"? A joke is not to be taken seriously; it may be in bad taste but can the gods not defend themselves? DO they really need human acolytes to spring to their defence?

Sham-Rocks

In the occult scene generally, there are many who look on themselves as being like Petros, St Peter, the rock on which the x'tain church is founded. They see themselves as the foundation rocks of their own branches of the occult. All too often they deserve the title of 'Petros'.

Perhaps because they are as hard as rock commercially, always looking for a monetary reward for their adherence to one path or another. Or, because they are immovable, even when they are proved wrong. Because they are just as thick and solid between the ears, or because they are rocks on which their particular path may flounder.

Some make TV appearances, some write books and/or articles. Some give talks at conferences, camps, symposiums, etc. Almost always they are whiter than white, good universally loving people. Yes! They probably polish their harps with Silvo and their wings are daily dusted with Pickerings Stardust No 3.

Many have grandiose titles – High Priest, High Priestess, Guru, Magister, Adeptus – or even, so help me, Master! Strangely, the ladies who approximate this degree are known as Lady, never as Mistress – even if they are someone's. How many of these titles are crutches for the ego I wonder?

Are such people genuine? Who am I to say? Who am I to judge? All depends really on their sincerity. As regards Wicca, as the practice of modern witchcraft in its many forms has now become known, there are many who are undoubtedly sincere. Some of the older adherents, those who practiced prior to the advent of Gardner and Sanders, have adopted and adapted innovations brought in by these gentleman. Not all,, but it has become necessary for some of them to accept titles such as High Priest and High Priestess – unknown to them before.

But many of those who refer to themselves generally as 'pagans' are of all kinds. Some of them, if they do not actually bring discredit on the Craft, do lower it on occasion to the point of making it a subject of public hilarity. Among these may be the ones who ensure the press is informed when they cast 'spells' on people, usually prominent people. Of course, not a *harmful* spell, merely a 'binding' spell. Why, oh why, do they not cast a self-inflicted binding–of wide elastoplast round their heads to cover their mouths. Why can't they utilise the occult injunction to 'Keep Silence'?

I heard of a lady who is alleged, at least by her partner, to be a High Priestess of a coven in the city where they reside. She gave a talk at an event organised by friends of her partner. At this venue she proclaimed during the talk that: "People who are overweight cannot be pagans."

What a remarkable statement. How wise the one who uttered these words. Rush off, all you pagans, and immediately consult your dietician, the new ruling deity of all pagan branches. I have heard also that one cannot be a Witch if one is disabled. How terrible. One day you are a Witch, the next you are involved in a road traffic accident and lose a leg. Don't use a broomstick as a crutch, you can no longer be a Witch.

The lady at the function would have been annoyed had someone stated that as the Craft is a fertility religion, basically only women who are built like women can be witches, let alone High Priestesses. That woman who could be mistaken for long haired, effeminate males cannot be Witches. Have you ever heard of a Mother Goddess or one of her representatives who had to bottle-feed her child, divine or otherwise?

But it is not only Witches whose noses we may be getting up.

Perhaps you are a shaman.

Let us look at sham-shamans.

Shamanism is a comparatively new bandwagon which many have jumped upon. At one time few in number, there are shamans (or alleged shamans of both sexes) to be found beating their drums, if not blowing their own trumpets, all over the land. For so many, how true the title sham-man. True shaman I have respect for because s/he has earned their title. So very many have earned nothing at all but amused contempt. But again, who am I to judge? This is *their* path. Faced with doubt they are so righteous in their indignation. But as Anton LaVey says in his Satanic Mass: "The angel of self-deceit is camped in the souls of the righteous."

Self-deceit is not the only kind. Some so-called shamans are wonderfully confident tricksters. I came across one once who had a great act: the Great Pretender indeed. Several youngsters thought he was a marvellous shaman indeed - for a while - until he left town and left them out of pocket. This shaman had a remarkable knowledge of Ameri-Indians. He was unaware that the 'totem poles' of many of these peoples are, in reality, either grave markers or a family history of the head of the family. Our modern European shamans often adopt, rather than are adopted by, totem animals and/or 'power animals'. I notice these are always eagles, bison, wolves, etc. I knew one alleged shaman whose totem would more appropriately have been a bed bug, a tapeworm or some other parasite. Qualities he had in abundance. Instead of a 'power animal' he would be more successfully identified with a 'power plant'. A loofah – like him, it is an excellent sponge!

Of course, shamans communicate with the spirits, sometimes the spirits of their ancestors. ... so do spiritualists. The dictionary states that a necromancer is one who communicates with the dead. It says nothing of evoking spirits to appear, either in ectoplasm or confusion, in the ritual magician's 'triangle of art' while s/he stands in a protective circle. It says naught about the necromancer being anything other than one who communicates with the spirits of the dead.

So spiritualists say: "We only contact the physical spirits of the dead if they wish to communicate and it has to be through a guide." All right! So their 'guide' graciously allows contact with the physical (bodily) spirits of the deceased. The bodily spirit, the 'low self' is the shell, well known to utilisers of the Qlipoth, as one of the inhabitants of that realm. It would appear then, that despite their protestations, these mediums may well utilise the Qlipoth.

What about ritual magicians? People pay great sums of money for old *grimoires* – grim indeed! A *grimoire* is, in effect, a handbook and that's all it is, despite the grandiose titling. One loony character swore he possessed the finest book of 'black magic' ever produced–*the Book of Ebon Bindings*. Black magic, indeed! It was produced in the USA by a games company; one of the *Dungeons and Dragons* variety, it bore a resemblance to a *grimoire* with demons of unpronounceable names and fearsome description.

The ritual magician stands in a protective circle – often two circles embellished with a pentacle, cups of 'holy' water, Hebrew characters, candles and, if s/he has read Dennis Wheatley, with bunches of foul-smelling grass. He then gestures like a demented demon, chants and/or proclaims names and/or words of power. He evokes what he hopes is the desired demon to appear in the 'triangle of art'. This triangle is marked some distance from the circle and is intended to restrain the demon. The magician then demands that the demon appear and if it doesn't, it is threatened by progressively stronger threats—even to the threat of turning the power of the Almighty against it!

I've heard of rejoicing in heaven but this must be the cause of pain in hell. The pain of aching from unstoppable side-splitting laughter. This powerful magician, uttering his terrible threats, is going to get the demon of his choice to appear in a *magically restricting triangle* while the powerful macho, robed and sword-armed magician cowers in a double circle, protected by candles, holy water, magical characters and herbs.

What of Dr Dee and Edward Kelly who 'discovered' Enochian, the language of the Angels. Not only did these extra-terrestrial beings teach them their language, Dee and Kelly had their fortunes told – which proved in the end to be somewhat erroneous. Much to the ladies' annoyance, the Angels decided that Dee and Kelly should swop wives. Well, I've heard some ploys used in 50 years of occult study and practice, but not even when President of a Chapter of Hell's Angels did I come across that one.

Philosophy & Opinion

Philosophy & Opinion

It should be understood that although Bob firmly held the philosophy and opinion that all Faiths were One, and all Paths led to the same Goal, he did not advocate what is now referred to as 'eclectic paganism'. What he did teach was the desire for knowledge and experience, regardless of source.

Each new experience was, however, studied *within* the confines of that particular religion, path or tradition. Each discipline was kept completely separate from each other – Craft : Ritual Magic : Oriental : Tradition : Mythos. It was only when a student had a thorough understanding of the tenets of each discipline were they encouraged to formulate them into their own individual system. In this his working methods closely resembled those described by Israel Regardie in *The Eye in the Triangle* of Crowley's own training methods as used in the A.A.

Acceptance

From *Phoenix* magazine: "When a man or woman accepts a particular religion, belief, or path–call it what you will–then s/he is certain that all others are wrong. They may *say* that others are entitled to their own beliefs, but give them some power and, no matter that they preach, they will exert that power to the utmost to control those who think even a little differently.

Protestant against Catholic; Sunni against Sufi; Hindu against Sikh; Gardnerian fundamentalist against 'New Age' Wiccan; Qabalist against Qliphotist – all have their followers who will try to force their beliefs down other people's throats.

Few seem genuinely able to accept that others have a path, a way, a system, which may be just as valid as their own. There is a saying of the Sufi that: "There are many paths to Allah as there are souls of men". But even here, among the followers on one path there will be differences. These may be minor differences, but they exist.

Every person is an individual and it was in recognition of this acceptance that the first multi-path coven was formed [the Coven of the Scales]. If all paths are acceptable with and despite their differences, there is less friction, less back-biting and more harmony.

Communication is necessary to all living species, though Western mankind in particular appears to be the only animal that suffers from compulsive and *unnecessary* communication. Not only is body language used, but he has to pollute decent silence with noise – and not only by voice. The Deities, being spiritual, communicate with mankind in various ways including thought. Only in myth and legend do the exalted Beings utilise vocalisation like manic thunder accompanied by bursts of heavy metal music!

Mankind, though, in the majority of his forms of group worship, finds it absolutely necessary to disturb the atmosphere as part of the service. Tibetans blow down several metre-long trumpets while Christians of various sects have organs which cause an aggravated assault on the ear. Although the fundamentalist variety abjure the organ, they demonstrate they are 'with it' by the use of guitar, clap and waving their arms while singing and writhing like demented dervishes. The last is a poor simile ... the dervishes known as the Whirling Dervishes are silent while performing their graceful dance. Many religions uses gongs and/or drums–as if afraid that unless the Gods' or Goddesses' attention is kept riveted to the performance, they will fall asleep and fail to listen.

With the usual cacophony produced, it must take superhuman hearing to decipher the pleas for forgiveness. Or the brownie-point-scoring, divine-ego-boosting, memory-jogging reminders to the deity of what s/he has created. Of how great s/he is; how powerful and, perhaps by these reminders, how forgetful! Of course, there is always payment required in the form of requests for help, mercy, etc. No wonder there are disasters to the human race, like plague, treatment-resistant tuberculosis, AIDS ... Could the deity be trying to communicate – to tell *us* something?

Despite mankind's long experience of using his vocal cords in a diversity of languages, he is not yet competent in expressing himself in a manner that can be fully understood.

For instance, Alex Sanders, the late King of the Alexandrian Witches, was ill for a while in the 1960s. Prayers for his recovery were said by members of at least one of his covens in Warwickshire. This coven produced a small newsletter for distribution among its members and although I was not a member I usually managed to obtain a copy. Alex duly recovered from his illness (with or without the Goddess's assistance). So much for forethought when communicating by newsletter – the next issue bore the exultant message: "The Goddess is good – Alex is better."

Now a strange form of communication exists between myself and a gentleman of Asian extraction. I am writing this article while sitting in a café on a Sunday afternoon – suspecting that this gentleman will soon come to bother me. He is a *sadhu*, a holy man, who openly proclaims to be a prophet. Of Sikh birth, he was educated at a Christian Mission School and has developed his own brand of religion which is compounded of Brahmanism and Christianity. The Sikh community and his extended family have taken over his family responsibilities and believe that "God has kissed him".

Personally, I think that, far from kissing him, the God of Discord has indecently assaulted him! He was first introduced to me some months ago, since when I am at risk whenever I go to the library or to this café to write. He asks me questions and I answer from my own small store of occult knowledge. Something, however, is very wrong with my powers of communication. A week or two later he is likely to recount to me the explanations I have given him, and assure me that: "God has told me this". It was news to me that I had attained the Godhead.

At times he is a damned nuisance, breaking into my privacy or conversations, but he cannot be insulted. He is always cheerful and I think he truly does, as he claims, love everyone as his brother or sister. In many ways he is an inspiration. The paths to wisdom and to knowledge of deity are many and varied. Even apprentice 'nuggets' can sometimes point the way and can be good at teaching us to control our worst emotions, as well as showing an example of tolerance. It may well be that even those whom we deem mad may be used by deity to communicate with us."

A Sideways View of Witchcraft

This is an extract from one of the Frater Asmodaeus Tapes ...

Many year ago, among his many pronouncements, the much venerated St Augustine said and wrote that: "Cleanliness is of the Witch and the Devil". Did the saint mean to imply that, though one may rot in hell, only those in heaven will stink? Thomas Becket was adjudged to be a saint because following his assassination (a very incompetent and highly unprofessional job by today's technical standards), his undergarments had to be cut from his body because they were welded to it by dirt and accumulation of dead lice.

In the 1200s, in England, a countrywoman took a gown to the river to wash it. She pulled out the lining of the pockets and washed the inside of the pockets in this way. It cost her life. Someone reported her cleanliness and, thanks to St Augustine' being a filthophile, she was hanged as being a Witch.

Witches of the Middle Ages are often described as casting evil spells to harm men and animals and to sink ships. They were said to worship the Devil and to make pets of cats, dogs, frogs, toads and bats. Who said this? Anyone who didn't want to be tortured. Women were the main targets. A man might like to be well hung but not by the neck from a gibbet. On whose authority were these things said about Witches? On the authority of the church, of course. All very unbiased. It's like accepting without question the view of the Roman Catholic Church as seen by the Rev. Ian Paisley, or the rights of the Palestinians by an Ashkanazi member of Beth Shin or Mosad.

We may be forgiven then for turning from the Middle Ages to look at those who today would call themselves Witches. During the period before the repeal of the Witchcraft Act in 1951, the practice of witchcraft was illegal. Groups or covens of Witches did exist though. They met in secret and little was kept in writing which might incriminate anyone, and certainly I know of no so-called *Book of Shadows* being kept. The alleged contents handed down from the Middle Ages when even the aristocracy rarely knew how to write, let alone the village wiseman or woman, are highly suspect indeed. At least this applied to Witches in Cheshire, Shropshire and North Wales whom I knew. After the repeal of the Act things began to really hum – almost as much as the christians of Augustine's day must have done. By now, of course, personal hygiene had been discovered and been sanctified by John Wesley, who defied Augustine by declaring that "Cleanliness is next to Godliness".

Upon the scene came Dr Gerald Gardner. He certainly livened up witchcraft from how I knew it. Despite calling the Craft a lunar faith with a moon goddess, he was a sun worshipper himself, being a nudist (now called naturalists). He was used to seeing naked bodies – so am I, but his were all living! The nudes I got my hands on were on the autopsy table.

He introduced the idea of working 'sky clad' though I've yet to see a Witch dressed in a cloud. Perhaps he was overly interested in sado-masochism because he also introduced scourging. Another of his innovations was the three degree system. Scourging was not done with a rubber hose so presumably not the origin of *his* third degree? He may have been influenced by the degree systems of some magical orders, or by the enth degree systems of some pre-repeal Witchcraft Act covens.

Despite the many criticisms about his new ideas, Gardner made modern witchcraft popular and built the bandwagon upon which so many have jumped.

He was followed by Alexander Sanders. Alex it was, I think, who introduced the idea of 'Witch Queens'. As a bi-sexual, in the days when homosexuals were not called gay but a number of other derogatory names, he probably knew many less than regal 'queens'. He introduced a form of Egyptian magic into his new witchcraft. He also introduced his Manchester sense of humour, a lot of publicity and drew a great deal of personal criticism and recrimination.

Modern witchcraft has changed out of all recognition since Gardner's day. Christianity, Judaism, Buddhism, and Islam, all have divided into mutually antagonistic sects and sub-sects. It is the same story with witchcraft. The christian sects differ as radically as the Holy Rollers, the Russian Orthodox Church, the Plymouth Brethren, the Church of England and the Salvation Army and yet all are christians. So now witchcraft is composed of many, all too frequently antagonistic, sects and sub-sects.

Even in these allegedly enlightened days there are still christians who see Witches as worshippers of the Devil and who believe that Witches attempt to do evil by the casting of spells and curses. Leaving cursing aside, where better to look so see what witchcraft is and who Witches really are, than in a dictionary? There witchcraft is defined as the casting of spells, evil doing, sorcery, magic and necromancy. The casting of spells and evil doing are self-evident in the eye of the beholder. It is true that Witches practice magic – but so do magicians and you can well be a magician without being a Witch. Wherever one looks in the dictionary, under magician, Witch or sorcerer, one word keeps appearing and is common to all–necromancer!

It may then be assumed that the true, traditional Witch is a necromancer. A necromancer, we read, is one who contacts and has communication with the dead. At last we are getting somewhere and with the authority of the *Bible* nonetheless. In the Old Testament the Jewish king called upon the Witch of Endor to summon up and have conversation with a dead Jewish prophet.

Does anyone today call up and hold converse with the spirits of the dead? Yes, but they deny being the real, traditional Witches and following the torture, hangings and burnings this is understandable. Who then are these true, genuine, vouchsafed-for by dictionary and *Bible*, Witches? Obviously they are the so-called spiritualists or spiritists. They, despite their denials are necromancers, therefore sorcerers and witches. Their High Priests and High Priestesses are the Mediums and no matter that they be small, large or outsize, they remain Mediums. Magic indeed! They converse with the dead. True, some call themselves *christian spiritualists* but, as I said, after the persecutions in the past who can blame them?

So! By a form of sideways thinking, we can uncloak that which covers witchcraft in its essentials; thus we can rend the veil and, without the aid of a King Witch or Witch Queen, we may ourselves become a *malleus malificarum.*

[i.e. *malleus* = a small crushing instrument; *malificarum* = wickedness, mischief. In other words someone who crushes the overt silliness in some Craft circles.]

Solitude

This extract, taken from an article first published in Sirius (June 1992) draws on the influence of Bob and Mériém's caving experiences, combining the two disciplines of potholing and magical practice.

"It is possible to find solitude even within a room filled with people, though it is easier in a room devoid of others. This has been discovered by many who have embraced transcendental meditation. It *is* possible to force one's attention away from extraneous noises which impinge from outside–voices, hammering, traffic, etc.

Perhaps the quietest place is in a cave or a disused mine – not the shallow cave of the hermit or Anchorite, where one still has the sound of the wind and rain, and a measurer of light. Further underground there are places where water does not drip or flow; where bats do not chatter; and where absolute darkness may be found. Here, if *meta menardi,* the cave spider and other smaller creatures are in residence, they will not be heard by you.

Initially, it may be difficult to relax completely. The imagination will produce light and/or sound. Perseverance is required. It may be of assistance at first to use a single candle–not to meditate on, but to be comforted by its light – until you are acclimatised to your surroundings.

In such surroundings, time appears to play tricks, even to the well-experienced speleologists and fodinaeologists. Accordingly, it may be as well to have an alarm clock with you, set for a particular time and covered well enough so that ticking cannot be heard – but no so well that you don't hear the alarm. Make sure that the roof of the chamber or passage is over a foot above your head, and preferably wear a helmet. A sudden and strident alarm in such surroundings can induce violent and involuntary levitation.

Once you have grown accustomed by practice to such surroundings, they become exceptionally good for developing communication with extra-terrestrial entities, intelligences and deities. Unless you are well-experienced in occult matters, it is advisable before relaxing to thoroughly steep your mind with the idea of the principal entity you would like to contact, and to seek that entity's protection from the attentions of any malicious spirits."

Throughout Bob's writing, references to 'extra-terrestrial entities' or 'intelligences' are a common theme. For the purpose of clarification, it should be taken to understand that he is referring to the discarnate entities that are frequently encountered on other psychic levels, i.e. entities not of this world or dimension, and of differing levels of intelligence.

East v. West? — Both are the same

A recent television programme recently offered evidence for the theory that Cernnunos, the stag-horned personification of the God of the Witches (or some Witches), was not European. As a God of the Western Tradition the idea is almost heretical but the evidence, however is quite believable. It shows that the representation of the Horned God which, after all, are few in number, have aspects that appear to be traceable by way of the decorations on artefacts on a long journey over many centuries to India.

Representations of the Lord, with one leg folded and accompanied by animals are alleged to have originated with depictions of Shiva, Brahmistic God of India. The route was traced by which the representations of Shiva travelled to Western Europe–perhaps as the result of trade over a great many years.

It was also shown that the Goddess of the Witches, or at least representations of Her, could also have come from India. If this is the case then as far as witchcraft is concerned, the religious aspect is not of the vaunted Western Tradition but a variation – one might even say a bastard form – of Brahmanism. I have no doubt that many 'traditional' Witches will strongly oppose this theory, even if they are unable to provide acceptable proof of the invalidity of their own theory. No one likes to have their beloved traditions questioned, let alone proof being produced to refute their veracity.

Does it really matter? All religions, when they grow, not only expand but also split into factions, like branches growing from the main trunk of a tree. This has happened across the world over time and pagans are no different. There are several forms of witchcraft which are frequently at odds with each other.

Is it not time that we ceased to define things as being of East or West? All traditions, all thought, all innovations, come from One Source. It matters not whether they travel from North, South, East or West. All have validity and all have a common origin, even if we are not able to immediately recognise it. East or West, they are the same, part of one planet. Impossible as it may seem at first without understanding, all Faiths are One.

Pagan Counselling

Recently, my wife and I were talking with a (not so young) lady who is 'co-ordinator' of a church-funded organisation that runs a coffee bar as a drop-in at a church in the City centre. She had advertised for volunteers to commence a counselling course to enable them to give advice on problems of various kinds.

We had, in the past, been known to have been of assistance to two previous officers who ran the drop-in with coffee-bar volunteers while they, themselves, dealt with any problems. The first, a Scots lady atheist, had moved to a similar post closer to home. The second, who had moved to take charge of a drug-abuse rehabilitation centre, was a young Jesuit priest. He had been in charge of a large RC City church but had the temerity to renounce celibacy and marry. The result was that he lost his living.

The relatively young (compared to us) lady sounded us out about becoming volunteers on her proposed counselling course.

We pointed out that our time is limited; not only are we on several local committees but we have a coven to run. In addition, we have articles to write and I have added to our burden by under-taking duties to assist the PF (Pagan Federation) in our region. In short, we declined.

During our conversation, however, it emerged that what we saw as counselling was not what the young lady had in mind. Her idea and, as she pointed out, she is qualified (having attended a 12-week course herself), is that counselling consists solely of listening to people talking about their troubles. Adding the occasional word or question to keep them 'talking it out'. The answers, she said, were in their own minds and to offer advice or help was 'interfering with their lives'.

To some extent, we agree with this – but can it be called 'counselling"? The Samaritans listen but do not get involved. The originator of the Samaritan movement, Chad Varah, said that the idea of the organisation was to provide a sympathetic, listening ear, not to counsel!

What then is counselling? According to the *Oxford English Dictionary*, Counsel, as a noun, means consultation, advice. The noun, counsellor, means advisor. An advisor is a person habitually consulted. Advise means to offer advice, to recommend.

It seems then, that according to the dictionary, a counsellor is *not* merely a listener who lets or encourages a person to 'talk things out' but one who is prepared to accept some responsibility for giving advice.

Listening plays a great part but must not, I think, become the be all and end all of counselling because some modern sages fear to take any responsibility and wish to hide behind the shield of non-interference. Six million Jewish people suffered as a result of a general policy of international non-interference..

History tells of monarchs and their counsellors. Our own Monarch has a Privy Counsellor, not to advise on the colour, length and texture of toilet paper, but to discuss and advise on matters of State. True, future history may tell of a group of listeners but these are not known as a council but a Cabinet. (This may be more appropriate now we are in the Common Market. The word in French means lavatory! A place where waste products are collected for dispersal.)

Advice given, or recommendations made may not always be for the best–and this is where experience counts. Of course, it may count and produce an incorrect answer but to abrogate all responsibility and merely listen may be rather like listening to a man shouting for help as he hangs from a cliff. To advise him where foot holds may be gained would obviously be to take responsibility and be seen as interfering.

Words do change their meaning. Maybe I'm just an out-of-date, old has-been. But better I think to be an old has-been than a young, never-will-be and those afraid to take responsibility will never really amount to much.

The articles I write under a demonic nom-de-plume are written under a name which is mine as a member of a certain Magical Order. It is not a means of avoiding responsibility, but of separating my more controversial articles from those of a lesser explosive content. Many, of course, know who the demonic writer is–but it also enables me to occasionally get two articles in one issue!

It is the practice in our coven (neither Gardnerian nor Alexandrian), *not* to Initiate to second degree and the priesthood until the potential second degree has some experience, not only of organisation and administration, but also of counselling. A second degree witch can 'hive' off and form a coven of their own. Of little use if the 'High Priesthood' cannot organise or administer. Nor if they are incapable of taking the responsibility of listening to a members' problem. Then, if the member cannot, after 'talking it out' see a way for themselves, offer advice on possible courses of action. The choice of action being for the member alone.

The title of High Priest, High Priestess, *Magister Templi*, Counsellor, or whatever, should not be merely a crutch for the ego–but should entail the realisation of, and the acceptance of, the responsibilities that go with the title.

"Uneasy lies the head that wears the crown" is a saying that is as true for the High Priesthood, and the High Grade or Degree

Initiate of a Magical Order, as it is for a monarch. The monarch reaps the material benefit of his/her responsibility. For the witch or magus, the reward is more insubstantial – spiritual, we hope, and not just egotistical.

Perhaps the way out of the dilemma of the changing meaning of words may be found in coining new terms. The counsellor who listens but takes no action might be said to practice 'passive counselling'. Those who elect to interfere when advice is requested may then be said to practice 'active counselling'. Thus are egos saved from affront and all can glory in the title of 'Counsellor', whether they have done a 12-week course to qualify, or have merely four decades of unqualified (and largely successful) practice.

If a pagan has a problem, can they be better understood by a non-pagan, psycho-therapist or counsellor, who is qualified but with little experience; or by an unqualified but experienced pagan counsellor?

Egg-sistence

Chaos has been said to be, or have been that peculiar state when: "The earth was without form and void, and darkness was upon the face of the deep". This was the state of inanimate chaos before life began. This state, awaiting activity and vitrification was symbolised world-wide by the ancients as an egg. The mundane egg, or the cosmic egg, they are both essentially the same. The passive and the formless within its shell, awaiting the initial act of creation. As Faber states, the egg came to represent not only the earth but also the Universe in its greatest extent [*Pagan Idol,* vol 1, p175].

According to Menu, the world was all darkness. It was indistinguishable and indiscernible. He states that the earth was in a profound sleep until Brahm, the self-existent, invisible god, using five elements and other glorious forms, made it manifest, perfectly dispelling the gloom. From his own essence he first created the waters and inspired them with the power of motion. It may be a good point to consider that so often in the supposedly primitive world the idea has lodged that it is from primordial waters that life arose. Modern scientific research tends to verify this ancient and widespread supposition!

Having created the waters Brahm, utilising the motion of the waters, produced a golden egg. "Like a thousand stars" within this golden egg was born the self-existent but unperceived, invisible cause–the future parent of all natural things. Brahma. For many years Brahma existed in the golden egg, meditating upon himself. At last he divided into two equal parts from which he fashioned the heavens and the earth, with the eight points at the world, the subtle ether and the permanent receptacle of the waters.

Well, that roughly is Maurice's translation. Sir William Jones has a slightly different version. According to him, "The sole, self - existent power, having willed to produce various beings from His own divine substance, first with a thought created the waters and placed in them a productive seed. That seed became an egg, bright and gold, blazing like the luminaries with a thousand beams, and in the egg was born Himself, in the form of Brahma, the great fore-father of all spirits."

Of course the Greeks had to get into the act – even in a play. Aristophanes wrote in his *Comedy of the Birds*, of black-winged Night, who with Chaos, Erebus and Tartarus was initially all that existed, produced an Aerial Egg. From this egg was born Golden-pinioned Phanmes–Love. Phanes, Aristophanes wrote: "The Great Universal Father begat our race out of dark Chaos, in the midst of wide spreading Tartarus and called us into light."

Thus, according to widespread ancient ideas, we have the egg representing Being simply, and Chaos, a void from which, by the will of Unity, the superlative force comes the influence of creation. This being designated among the Greeks variously as, 'The Universal Father', 'the Golden-pinioned Love', 'Phanes' and 'the Egg-born Protogones' (who later became the Roman Jupiter).

In Egypt, the Universal Creator was known variously as Ptah, Atum and Thoth. To the Indians, the 'Father of the Universe', the

Great Parent of Rational Creation was Brahma. The Chinese has similar ideas to those of India. The view of the Chinese was that before Creation there was Chaos in the form of an inconceivably vast egg. Though for a period before Creation 'inconceivably' might be the wrong adjective to use. This Chaotic Egg contained within it the principals of all things and the act of Creation was the vivification of the egg.

So we are left with the question, which came first, the Creation or the egg?

[1st July 1994]

Scientific Fairy Tales?

Anyone professing a belief in the existence of 'The Little People' in public is likely to be considered to be suffering from a mental condition of some kind. In our modern, scientific world, such creatures are deemed to be the subject of myth and folklore, rather like animals depicted in books intended for very young children.

Good and well-educated scientists, however, may be found who, while demanding 'scientific proof' of other claims, devoutly believe that the Creator of All, was prepared to impregnate a young woman in Judea, allowing this spirit to take on human shape, eat, breather and excrete like any other child–and later man. There is no 'scientific proof' that this startling series of events actually took place, yet these educated people believe that they did – whilst denying any possibility of the existence of creatures which are mentioned in one form or another in the folklore of almost every branch of the human race. This is truly a case of 'blind faith'.

But do such creatures exist? I doubt if they exist as traditionally described–like fairies with wings and wearing diaphanous dresses; and dwarves, all in late middle-age and wearing long nightcaps. Yet the stories abound of creatures appearing to humans in such guises. How can this be possible ? Let us, without the assistance of the 'eye of faith', examine some possibilities.

We can safely assume that all these multifarious creatures of folklore and tradition are non-human. They may be spiritual beings. Perhaps they exist in our Plane of Existence but are normally unseen. Is this all nonsense? Viruses can still not be seen by humans; only their shadows can be seen by the use of an electron microscope. Sub-viral life cannot be seen at all. Bacteria can only be seen by the use of a microscope. But since they have been isolated, fixed and stained, and thus seen, their physical existence has been accepted by humanity in general.

To operate the astral microscope and study these and many other formerly 'non-existent' creatures, alleged to be figments of the imagination of theorists (and psychics), we have to utilise the sense of sight. If we are without sight we could not prove their existence. Sight is a strange sense. Some of us have long sight, some have short sight. Some of us can see auras. Some see more colour shades than others. Some of us are colour blind.

With the assistance of technically produced devices people can see by way of infra-red wavelengths of light. Could it be that some people are able to see other creatures which are invisible to the majority? With technology, could we see these creatures? It may be that children can see such creatures, but swiftly learn to hide the fact rather than be punished for lying, or accused of having too vivid an imagination. They cease to wish to see that which brings them trouble and they allow that part (or dimension) of their sense of sight to atrophy.

Why should such creatures assume human shape and wear clothing? Is it because they wish to appear in the recognised and acceptable form to humans? The gnome will appear in the form in which he will be recognised; the fairy with wings—thanks to the illustrations in children's books. To a Burmese villager, who has not seen these Western books, the *nats,* or tree spirits do not manifest in human form, wearing a loin cloth.

It may be that the creatures such as those we know as elves, fairies, gnomes, etc do not inhabit the same Plane of Existence as us, but a dimension which is only fractionally apart from ours, allowing access, one dimension to another, even perhaps physically. It may be that the inter-access between the dimensions was

easier in the past – before man interfered and changed the atmosphere with emissions of carbon monoxide and sulphur fumes.
According to Islam, before mankind inhabited the Earth, it was inhabited by creatures, it says in the Holy Qur'-án, created of 'intensely hot fire'. This is interesting, as the Earth was once extremely hot, and the only other basic substance, other than carbon of which is living material can be made as far as we know, is silicon. A creature whose body is silicon-based could exist in very high temperatures. These creatures, who are the former inhabitants of our world, are the *djinn*, the Elementals of Fire.

There may be far more to the old folk-tales, the legends of traditions than is generally accepted because of lack of scientific proof. Is that because the 'scientist' is not prepared to investigate with an open and unbiased mind?

Food of the Gods

There is an old occult adage: "As above, so below". This is intended to imply that the events of the Macrocosm are reflected or repeated in the Microcosm. That which is done in heaven is also done on Earth. This happy state of affairs can cause some alarming trains of thought to be engendered. Do the gods and goddesses eat? Do they wage war on one another? Do they lie, cheat and steal from each other? Do they grow old and die?

Our Earth is filled with many types of creatures, not just humans. These different types of creature utilise many kinds of food. The herbivores have evolved to convert the 'bodies' or parts of plants to usable energy. Carnivores have evolved to having the ability to convert the bodies of herbivores to a form of energy they can utilise. Omnivores are able to convert both flesh and plants. It is all a matter of converting one form of energy to another form. If this is the case, the 'below' must be the case 'above'. It has long been a religious practice to offer deities food and drink of the kind consumed by the person making the offering. It would be foolish for a plant to offer mineral salts and sunlight to an animal. An offering plants to a carnivore is unlikely to find the offering acceptable.

What do the gods eat? What is the food the Gods have evolved to utilise? We have a clue in *Genesis* where is states quite categorically that the God of the Old Testament was a meat-eater: *"Abel was a keeper of sheep, but Cain was a tiller of the ground. And in the due process of time it came to pass, that Cain brought of the fruit of the ground an offering unto the Lord. And Abel, he also brought of the firstlings of his flock and of the fat thereof. And the Lord had respect unto Abel and to his offering: but unto Cain and to his offering he had not respect."*

On the other hand, could it be that they use the energy of emotion? If this is the case, it could explain many things. Ants milk aphids and protect them. Men keep livestock for what they provide. Man also improves certain of his stock to provide for specific needs – less fat, more wool, etc. Could it be that the gods farm mankind? What could man provide, and how could his strains be improved?

Mankind may provide emotion of a higher quality than that generated by animals. Animals can provide the emotional energy of fear, sexual desire, etc, but man can provide so much more, and slightly different varieties from the norm. Slight differences may engender slight variations in emotional energy wavelengths, just as boiling and baking can produce different tastes to beef.

Thought itself may be food for the gods. The thoughts and emotions of the various types of sexual deviant are different in some ways from those of the normal practitioner. The same may be said of the masochist, the sadist, and the sado-masochist. How far could our thoughts and emotions be manipulated?

Animals rarely fight to the death over territory or breeding rights. Men fight over territory which, once gained, often confers little on the majority doing the fighting. Men, and women, will on occasion kill for love. Mankind may be just a number of prize herds which are bred for our divine owners to manipulate – not just in the case of wars but in humdrum, everyday situations which have some emotional content. Wars may be reserved for some cosmic banquet, while everyday emotions. Provide every day food.

How are the strains improved by these divine herdsmen? They

are improved by increasing the apparent intelligence of certain creatures. They devise new weapons of destruction, new tools, new religions, new cultures. All are good for producing emotions of all kinds. As the gods breed and multiply, so their food supply increases its population and traumas. Does this make you think ... Does it get you annoyed ... Does it cause you to violently disagree?

Good! It might provide some deity with a snack!

Occult Jesters

The medieval jester, in parti-coloured hose, cap and bells is a well-known figure and appears in a pack of playing cards as 'the joker' and in the Tarot as 'the fool'. In modern card games a player can double the score by playing their Joker and, in this way, is perhaps unconsciously giving credit where it is actually due.

For the Joker or Jester is, in effect, wearing a disguise. As that other form of Jester, the circus clown, has a painted expression hiding his true face, so the medieval Jester at court hid his true worth under a show of foolishness and levity. The official Jesters lasted a long time; the last nobleman's Jester in England, 'Maggoty Johnson', was a contemporary of my grandmother and a very astute man. Although known as the King's or the Lord's Fool, they were anything but foolish and frequently anything but impoverished. One King's Fool endowed a London hospital from his earnings as a wise fool.

Why a fool? Because a fool is not accountable for his speech or actions. In the good old days, servants were looked upon as part of the furnishings and their presence, except when needed, went almost unnoticed. Things were said in the presence of servants which would or should not be uttered in the presence of others.

As a fool could not be brought to account for his speech or actions, he was in a privileged position. A King's Fool could say what he liked to the King without fear and was therefore someone the King could trust to tell him about things as they truly were, not as he would like to hear them. The Jester kept close to the King or Lord, ostensibly because he could make them laugh with his wit or antics.

He could, being a fool, go anywhere, almost without question, which put him in the position of hearing and seeing many things that might interest his master. A King needed to be aware; to expect rebellion, regicide or subversion and one of the few he could trust was his fool. Better to put his trust in a clever, observant fool, not afraid to speak his mind, than a self-seeking friend.

In the Islamic world, the mystics known as the Sufi, the 'witches of Islam', refer to themselves 'the Fools' because the mullahs and imans consider themselves to be wise men. There is a Sufi story which tells of a donkey which all its working life was employed in carrying loads of books to the University. At the end of its working life, was this the wisest donkey, or the most learned donkey of all those in the town?

In the occult world, foolishness and jesting are sometimes used as camouflage. The majority of non-occultists and indeed many non-discerning occultists, look on these people as fools, clowns or actors with little actual occult knowledge. They see them as 'dabblers' at best or, at worst, a great danger to the credibility of the occult per se. The discerning see through and beyond the superficial attitudes of such *jesters*. Sometimes, even the magical names they adopt, or the names given to them by others and in which they revel, serve their camouflage.

The Master Therion (Greek = The Beast) was one of the many names adopted by Aleister Crowley but he also assumed the name of 'the Great Beast' and enjoyed the name given to him by the newspapers of 'The Wickedest Man in the World'. Like some earlier writers of occult works, he had a tendency to impart *dis*-information to his readers. This was most cleverly done and an excellent method of keeping true knowledge from those who blindly accept, whilst being clear to those who could discern the real meaning behind his words.

An obvious name for an occult trickster is that of the Norse god, Loki. Loki was originally a god of the hearth fire, the Norse quivalent of the Roman goddess Vesta. The hearth fire gives, light, warmth and comfort – but poorly tended it can go out, or it can burn and cause destruction. Whichever it is to be, depends on those who observe the fire and understand it. Loki later became known as the god of mischief and negative energies.

There are some Initiates who assume the name of Loki; their words, spoken or written may appear to be designed to cause mischief and may, by some, be seen as evil. Others, however, less blinded by assumption, and with a higher quality of understanding gain from teaching.

Asmodaeus is generally known as the demon of lust and the second husband (after Adam) of Lilith. An earlier demonic dictionary gives him rather different attributes. Lust, however, is not always sexual; there can be a lust for truth, for knowledge, for understanding, etc. Occult jesters who assume the name of a demon may well do so knowing that they will be misjudged by those of lesser understanding. Like Loki's, their words may cause annoyance and discord. Those same words may give a different person (apart from amusement), an insight into other meanings and/or possibilities.

Frater Asmodaeus is only part of the hologram that makes up the author. Look at his writings and you may envisage a particular person. Look at the writings of Fetisha, Morticus, Ophidia, Aius Locutius, or any of the other names (including my given name) under which I write and you will, in most cases, imagine a different personality. Every man and every woman is a star with many arms pointing in different directions. Asmodaeus has assumed the function of a goad, to prick the bubbles of self-delusion and pomposity acquired by so many on the occult world. This is not only a world of illusion but also of hypocrisy.

To recognise and acknowledge one's own hypocrisy indicates that a step has been taken towards awareness; to have peeled off the outer skin of the onion of understanding. But the onion is composed of many layers and what lies beneath the mask of the clown?

Thus the occult joker or fool may assume a camouflage that may last a lifetime – only penetrable by the truly discerning. Alen Sanders, of happy memory, was one of these jesters. On the surface he appeared a fool, a charlatan, playing up to the press and bringing upon himself the wrath of those who considered themselves more knowledgeable.

So knowledgeable that they were like those spoken of in the Holy Qur'án, and considering themselves to be wise and yet "are as the blind, leading the blind, and though the truth be put plain before them, still they cannot see".

Is it better to be a fool, an occult jester with insight, or a wise person who is blind?

Light

Magazines and books of an occult nature should all seek to cast light and give illumination. Like old-fashioned lamps they need to be replenished with oil. The oil, and indeed the wicks are the articles and typescripts submitted for publication.

True, wicks occasionally have to be trimmed – especially mine.

Without oil and wicks in sufficient quantity the light will fade and grow dim. Darkness, the black night of ignorance, will commence its insidious encroachment.

Some 2,300 years ago, in the Acropolis in Athens, there used to stand a golden lamp. The gold lamp had been designed by the sculptor Callimachus. It was a famous object in its day and was reputed, once filled with oil and lit, to be capable of burning continuously for a year. Where is it now? Probably the gold was melted down and recycled long ago. Its light no longer shines, the Acropolis is a ruin, but it is still remembered.

Man-made light is only an auxiliary source of illumination. Knowledge, understanding and wisdom are derived from the God and Goddess.. They allow auxiliary sources on a temporary level in the form of verbal teaching, books and magazines. The effects of these may be long-lasting like the golden lamp of Callimachus. But these auxiliary sources of light can only generate illumination, or at least spread the light as long as the wicks and oil are available.

Writers are mortal. They do not last forever. They, like the wicks and oil need to be replaced in time. Lamps will only give illumination for as long as we let them. It is a boost to the ego to have your work published, but is a greater boost to think that your words may cast a little light, perhaps if only by stimulating thought.

It has been said that the pen is mightier than the sword. It may indeed be sharper than the magician's sword – and the sword is basically a destructive weapon.

Don't hide your light under a bushel, let it shine out and provide oil and/or wicks for those lamps of knowledge –the occult publishers.

Bob Clay-Egerton: 24th May 1993

Magical Practice

Magical Practice

On the subject of actual magical practice and technique, there was (perhaps not surprisingly), very little written for the public domain. Occasionally, a small piece appeared that contained some very important magical truths, such as this one that appeared in *Phoenix* magazine.

To Keep Silent

"Occasionally I am admonished by other occultists for 'teaching' by describing some of the mistakes that I have made in the past, and their results. The admonition is because the complaining occultists think that, by admitting that I can and *do* make mistakes, and do foolish things, I lower the esteem which magic and/or witchcraft may be held by newcomers to the occult.

With this evaluation, correctly or incorrectly, I disagree. Magic, whether performed by Witch, Cabbalist, Vodois, Ngonga, shaman, ritual magician or Uncle Tom Cobbley and all, is independent of the necessity of the esteem of any human. It may lower the esteem in which I am *personally* held, but if so, then so mote it be! I am not a deity, or laity, nor am I Pope. I am by no means infallible.

Not only do I regret many of my mistakes, though so have given rise to much merriment, I accept them. It is my hope that I have learned from them. Further, I hope that by recounting them, three things might occur: One, that those who hear of my mistakes may thus be prevented from making similar ones.

Two, that the realisation that I *can* make such mistakes, usually because of the possibilities connected with the actions or words, will have a deterrent effect. It may deter the newcomer from accepting blindly 'the truth' in everything I say. Based on the false assumption that nearly five decades of occult study and the acquisition on the way of ego-boosting titles, grades and ranks in occults groups, must be so. Experience does not always bring knowledge. Study does not always bring understanding. Age and 'High Office' do not necessarily bring wisdom.

Thirdly, the newcomer to the occult may realise that it is necessary to continue despite making mistakes and regret, even feelings of guilt. The God and Goddess chastise for our own good as well as bless; and their chastisement is itself, eventually to be seen as a blessing.

To keep silent when by speaking you might prevent distress may be wrong. However, sometimes it may be best to remain silent after your initial words have been rebuffed. As an example, may I recount a tale concerning the late King George VI when he was a child.

In those days the rule was; and it had some advantages, that 'a child should be seen and not heard'. This was especially the case at meal times. One evening at dinner, the future monarch was sternly admonished for attempting to break into the conversation and gain the attention of King Edward VII. After dinner, King Edward asked what had occasioned his display of bad manners. The young Prince George is reputed to have replied: "I was merely going to inform you, Grandfather, that there was a caterpillar in your salad. It does not matter now, you have eaten it!"

The decision regarding the keeping of silence is, and must always be, a personal one, irrespective of tradition, rules and regulations."

Left Hand or Right Hand Path

Despite the historical and innocent designations of left and right to the two major Tantric streams, over time it has become common belief that those who follow the Right Hand Path do good by working for the benefit of others, while the followers of the Left are selfish, working only for the good of themselves. It is, however, not quite so clear cut as that.

The LHP practitioner does not usually stick his/her nose in someone else's business, interfering with the natural course of events in a person's life by, say, healing. Especially if this is not specifically asked for by the one to be healed. The RHP practitioner, by all accounts, does 'good' in order to assist their own spiritual development. Does this not mean that the 'good' is done for the benefit of the RHP practitioner, and is therefore selfish—and thus LHP practice by the standards of the RHP? In not interfering, the LHP practitioner could be said to be doing 'good' and therefore actually following the standards attributed to the RHP.

Invocation & Evocation

This extract was taken from Bob's hand-written script for one of his tutorials.

Invocation and evocation are terms which are frequently misused, due to the misunderstanding of their exact meaning. Invocation might be best remembered and distinguished from evocation from its first two letters—I and N—forming the word IN. This is because in the correct use of the term, the witch or magus calls upon a god or goddess to possess him or her. To take over the invoker's body so that s/he *becomes* that god or goddess and possesses the power of that deity.

This means we take the god or goddess into ourselves and give up, albeit temporarily, the control of our body by inviting the deity to take control. The taking over, or coming in, is the operative element, so it is simple to remember that Invocation is the plea for deity to come in. Here we must understand and accept that only possession by the required deity or god-power is the intended result.

In modern practice, many invokers call, not only upon a deity but on some lesser entity. And it is not always realised that it is not absolutely necessary for a god, goddess, or lesser entity to be specifically called upon by word of mouth. It may be sufficient to change the wavelength of the magus's being to a receptive state by means of meditation, trance or self-hypnosis. These states which, apart from meditation, can be induced by rhythmic drumming, chanting, flashing lights, singing, dancing and numerous other means. A more Western example may be found in some of the fundamentalist christian sects where a build up of emotion can result in the phenomenon known as "speaking in tongues."

It is not, therefore, necessary to *intentionally* invoke a particular entity; it is sufficient to put the mind into a state suitable to *allow* possession by another entity. To do so is to open a psychic doorway through which an extra-terrestrial intelligence may enter a mind suitably, if only temporarily, adapted so that it may control the earthly body.

The danger can arise that the person who puts him/herself into this state (or allows themselves to be put into a suitable state) for possession, may have no control over what level of extra-terrestrial intelligence takes the advantage.

In contrast, in rites evocation, the wand or, in the case of the magician, more usually the sword, is the primary weapon used; although strictly speaking, the sword is not an element weapon. This is because the evoker is not intending to be possessed. Evocation is, correctly, the calling *on,* not deities but on lesser entities or extra-terrestrial intelligences such as demons. Though less than deities, these entities may yet be as powerful and/or dangerous.

The invocation of a god or goddess into a Circle into which the invoker is standing is because the Circle is a symbol of Unity: also the symbol for an entrance, a gateway, a chalice, cup or 'receiving vessel'. It becomes, in effect, the symbolic outer rim of the receptacle, while the symbolic receiving vessel in the invoker. Of the elemental weapons, the chalice is of prime importance in invocation ceremonies. [This will explain why Bob went into such detail over the selection of the chalice in Know Thy Weapons – page 15].

Thus the wand, or sword, is intended to keep such entities separate form the evoker. The magician usually stands in a protective circle and calls upon the desired entity to manifest in a specially prepared, restrictive triangle of conjuration. In this way, it may also be said that the guardians of the quarters are evoked to guard the Circle from outside.

The *invoker* then, calls IN a god or goddess, to bring their macrocosmic force to the human microcosm, but the *evoker* becomes the symbolic macrocosm and calls forth the elemental intelligences to manifest in the microcosmic triangle.

What is the summoner to do with the power gained? It can't be kept permanently because the human body is not designed or intended for such a purpose. No! One discharges the power in some way by using it to animate a thought form to perform some task. It may be transferred to a weapon or talisman in the form of a charge; or it may be passed on to members of a group. The power *must* be used or transmitted in some way as only by its use is it effective.

A charged talisman or weapon, however, is like a storage battery. The power it has received can be discharged when necessary to some purpose which eliminates the need for a complete invocation every time the power is needed. Atavars of gods and goddesses, and high grade Adepts may not need a ceremony to invoke their deities.

With such people it may be accomplished in seconds and the power sent out or 'earthed'. *This can be a little disconcerting to an inexperienced witch or magician who witnesses it.* With magical evocation it is necessary before attempting to control the lesser entities, to invoke and be possessed of the power of a deity. Above all it must be remembered that one must have sincerity of intention.

Underground Initiation

This piece, written by Bob, dated 15th February 1993, describes one of the methods used in Old Craft, location permitting.

Initiation may be into anything which has about it mysteries, secrets, skills or 'tricks of the trade'. One can be initiated into the art of garrotting with a cheese wire, or a length of wire from a piano or cello. (The A or E string usually, though the E string tends to be less easily recoverable after use.) Or, in these more peaceful days, one may be initiated into the mysteries of the computer/word processing, which is less disturbing to the conscience in later years.

Initiation is, in effect, a form of re-birth from an old style of life to a new one. Usually one with more responsibility and more awareness. Of course, when you look at the behaviour of some who are alleged to have passed into the initiatory stage, you may wonder about the veracity of this.

It is not unusual for initiation rites to be performed with some form of ordeal attendant to them. As birth is an ordeal so, in many cases, is the re-birth of initiation. (Thinkers can now start worrying about their possible future tribulations attending re-incarnation.)

The pseudo-initiation rites of industry can prove humiliating, dangerous and, on occasion, fatal. The apprentice cooper, having served his time, is expected to build a large cask by himself. This is then examined by a Master cooper. If the work is deemed expert enough the apprentice enters the cask and has the lid secured; he is then rolled about in it before emerging, somewhat bruised, as a recognised cooper. The cask that he had made and in which he is voluntarily imprisoned, represents the uterus and the rolling about represents the passage down the birth canal before he emerges to a new life with his new status.

In the old days of British coal mining, the official initiation period consisted of 28-30 days working underground, under the supervision of an experienced miner. If satisfactory, the trainee then received a declaration that he was judged competent. This was issued underground and usually written with a stub of pencil on an official slip of paper. I was both amused and honoured, after many years as leader of a cave rescue organisation and a rather well-known fodinaeologist, (a student of mines and mining as a specialised branch of industrial archaeology), to receive one of these pieces of paper.

Unofficial initiation rites are practiced in some mines, often performed by a small group of morons who gang up on a new trainee. Although fighting underground is a criminal offence, my previous military training of a rather specialist nature came to my aid and I was not 'initiated', nor was any further attempt made to initiate me, though the pit's 'accident' rate had a temporary rise, blamed appropriately enough on carelessness.

Some, so-called, primitive people send their young, would-be warriors out alone to fend for themselves for the space of a 'moon', i.e. from one new moon to the next. A case of the survival of the fittest. The Masai used to grant manhood only to a child who faced a lion alone, armed only with a shield and a spear. Other native people build a tunnel of boughs and leaves, to simulate the passage of the birth canal. The initiates who have passed the previous tests enter at one end of the tunnel, while their elders beat the framework, sometimes stabbing through it with spears, as they make their way through to emerge at the other end as men.

The girls do not necessarily have it any easier. They are usually removed from the village for at least a month to be instructed in the women's mysteries while living in isolation from parents and friends with old women who they serve as servants for this period of time.

The idea of re-birth implies death and burial before the birth of the new personality and I have been more than a soldier and miner in this life. Normally, I would not interfere with anyone's initiation rites if they are those of an occult group. However, when I took over as departmental head of the mortuary department (which was a sub-department of the Pathology department) in a very large hospital I thought it necessary on discovering that a young porter was to be 'initiated' into the portering staff by being placed for half an hour on a body tray in one of the 'fridges among the corpses.

I forbade the practice, not just to save the young man from a bad experience, though I understand that some people are afraid of death and even the dead. My arguments were that (1) he may have been affected by the cold since the temperature of the body fridges being a steady 2 degrees above freezing. (2) that it did not show respect for the deceased occupants and (3) that though I might risk contamination while opening a corpse during a post-mortem examination, I was not prepared to risk a young man's health, since there is a constant flow of air from the fridge unit through the banks of trays. I do not believe in pulling rank when reasonable argument can cause the offender(s) to save face and it saves issuing direct orders.

The 'into the grave and back' idea is still used by some occult groups. With some it is perfunctory, with others less so. In the 'less so' cases it can have a profound affect. Examples of the more perfunctory sort may be found in the initiations carried out in Yorkshire, Derbyshire and Cheshire.

A particular group in North Yorkshire used a cave in a dale running along one side of Whernside, one of the famous three peaks of Whernside, Ingleborough and Pen-y-Ghent. The cave, Yordas Cave, is a disused small show cave. It is named after the giant Yordas who was reputed to have made his uncomfortable home there. Uncomfortable because the smaller, second chamber contains a waterfall. This is convenient for drinking water or for a cold shower–remarkably cold in winter. My wife, Mériém, once resembled the god Shiva by having blue skin after showering there.

The main, first chamber is quite large with a sandy, relatively boulder-free floor. The noise of the waterfall you can get accustomed to but when the snow thaws, or there is a thunderstorm, or prolonged rain, it can become inches deep in water. Not up to the roof like Sleets Gill, or Mossdave Cavern of tragic memory, but not suitable for comfortable habitation.

I have known a group from Glossop in Derbyshire to use one of the nearby disused flagstone mines on Kracken Edge. It was not so much 'The Kracken Wakes' as 'The Roof Falls' and they were lucky. Not only that the mine did not truly become a grave, but that most of the rescue team were occultists – and not too surprised at having to rescue a young, naked lady from behind the fall in a most unsuitable and bloody dangerous mine.

Since the National (Dis)Trust took over the Cheshire powerzone, archaeological site and beauty spot at Alderley Edge, there have been changes which have affected occultists who have, for many decades, used this ancient and important site. Camping and the lighting of fires have been banned. When the by-laws were first posted up in the woods, it was not only the occultists who were intrigued to read that it was forbidden for anyone to "land a sea-plane, except in cases of emergency". It would be a magician indeed who would attempt to land a sea-plane in Alderley Woods, or on the boulder-strewn treeless slopes.

The entrances to many of the mines have been filled in. The Wood Mine, once extensively used by occultists because of its large chambers has been closed, except for access via a shaft with a locked lid – which will by now have probably sealed the fate of the bats that lived in the mine. Access is controlled, not by fodinaeologists, but by a caving club. Still open is the CCH Mine, the copper and cobalt mine which is in reality an exploration level dating from the mid-1800s. It has just outside the entrance the 'Icene Stone' a large bunter sandstone block which was frequently used as an altar.

In the past, the CCH Mine was often used for initiation rituals. Though the entrance is quite high, it soon drops to a height of about 6 feet and narrows to a width of around 4 feet. At the end one has to get onto one's hand and knees to enter a small, sandy chamber, roughly oval and about 6 feet wide, ten feet long and five feet high. At each end of the oval is a small silted up passageway which, for ritual purposes, simulates a womb.

Alas, access is also now unavailable to the 'Great Adit'. This flooded passageway runs from the foot of a hillside under the main part of the Edge. Once connecting by shafts, the side entrance to the CCH Mine, the Engine Vein Mine reached as far as the end of a mine in the Artist's Lane Valley. In places, the walls of this passage are green (malachite) and the roof blue (azurite) from the cupiferous arsenical salts. The passage, as late as 1948, was traversed by means of a wooden boat, blunt at each end, no bows at all. In one form of initiation, a pre-initiated was carried down this passage for about three-quarters of a mile to where the passage widened slightly and it was possible to land on a sandy bank.

The pre-initiated was landed on this bank and provided with a quarter inch of candle. The candle was lit and the boat departed, leaving the postulant alone in what was soon to become total darkness. The experience of over 24-hours alone in total darkness, under many feet of solid rock, in utter silence, with even the water not moving, is perhaps the nearest thing one can come to what equates with having passed, with perception, into death and been buried. When, finally the water begins to move, you hear the slight sounds of the approaching boat and at last see, far off, the faint glimmer of light, you have become a new person. You are, in some ways, re-born.

All initiations are, in a sense self-initiations, for realisation, awareness comes from within the initiate's sub-conscious. Ritual and the presence of witnesses, human and/or spiritual is only necessary to assist in conditioning the mind to an acceptance of a new state of being. Of all rituals, those which more closely symbolise the death of the former personality, and the birth of a new one, are perhaps the most effective. Of such rituals, the actual immurement for a period underground, may well be the most effective and longest lasting.

Qliphotic Qabalah

The Jews claim to be God's chosen people. My wife is half-Jewish. Does this mean she is only half chosen, or that God can't make up his mind and is still dithering? No matter, she chose me. It's not often a Jew makes a bad bargain, so the non-Jewish part must have exerted an influence nearly forty years ago. God's chosen people obtained much knowledge from their neighbours centuries ago, especially from the Egyptians and the Sumerians. It was probably the Sumerians who originated the system which has become known as the Hebrew Qabalah.

The name is naturally erroneous. Qabalah, no matter how it is spelt, means a system. Not any particular system. One can have a numerology Qabalah, a harmonic Qabalah, a colour Qabalah, even a sexual Qabalah. What is termed generally *the* Qabalah is the system of working that utilises the representation of the so-called Tree of Life. This Tree has ten sephiroth (singular sephirah), three of them – three being a magical number, at the top and above the 'hidden' or eleventh sephirah.

It is this hidden sephirah which is referred to by some as the Abyss, the entrance to the realm of the Qlipoth and the so-called Tree of Death. When mentioned at all in literature, or by word of mouth, the Qlipoth is usually described as evil, the Abode of the Shells of the Dead, of demons, elemental spirits, etc. I have asked occultists who warn against the Qlipoth how they *know* it is evil, and/or destructive? The usual answer is that they have been told this by their teacher, or they have read that it is so.

When, on occasion, I have managed to meet the teacher of this wisdom, and ask from whence has this knowledge of the Qlipoth come? I am told: "This is what I was taught." "It is written by eminent occultists" or "It is age-old knowledge." There we appear to have it. The same types of answer one usually gets with other Qabalahs, other systems of the occult.

Well, now! Age-old knowledge is it?: It was centuries, if not age-old knowledge that the Earth was flat. Some people still believe this to this day. So it was written by eminent men. I remember reading the words of an eminent scholar and scientist, a member of the Royal Society, who vouchsafed to the world the information that: "Snow is composed of a particle of fire and a particle of water". As a child I made snowballs to throw at cook and the gardener and I well remember that there was a sensation of burning heat when compressing snow. The snow, if held in the hand turned to water.

I can see how the eminent scientist came to his conclusion, and I am not a particle physicist, but so it was written in a scientific paper. Another case of "So let it be written. So let it be believed". What is in print must be believed, you know. The blindly accepting teacher is no better than the person who taught him and this may perpetuate a lie for centuries.

I can see that people do not care to question. It implies self-aggrandisement, conceit, inflated ego. It can cause punishment in the young, estrangement and unfriendliness for the mature. This is for those who openly challenge statements. By all means listen. By all means read - *but do not accept blindly!* Can the Eskimo know the heat of the tropics or the native of the Congo know the cold of the Arctic without experiencing them? The Qabalist cannot know what the Qlipoth truly is, good, evil or indifferent, without experimentation and experience.

The Qlipoth may be the sub-conscious, the Ygdrassilic Well of all thought, ideas and inspiration which nourishes the Tree of Life. Leaves and branches deprived of nourishment wither and die.

Do not, by blind acceptance of any system, deprive yourself of nourishment.

Candle Magic

Candle Magic is relatively simple and inexpensive but it cannot be adequately dealt with in a short article. However, one or two hints and pieces of advice can be given.

Preparation

As with anything which you want to be successful, you must prepare both yourself and your equipment. First of all THINK about EXACTLY what you want to accomplish by your magical act. It's no good changing your mind half way through the act. Then get together everything you are going to need, candles, matches, candlesticks, etc. Run through the ritual a couple of times as a 'dry run' and be sure that you have enough room to move in case you are going to be moving the candles. Be sure nothing stands a chance of catching fire. You're not an occultist on Australian TV; you're not going to risk scorching your sensitive parts!

Action

Rituals vary and you can make up your own. This is why dry runs are of use; you can establish a pattern of movement and thought, even speech which helps to focus your thought, or at least to reinforce it. A very simple ritual is to 'cleanse' the working area by using a 'banishing' ritual before casting a circle for the operation, invoking the quarter guardians to prevent unwanted interference, setting up your candles, making your wishes known, lighting the candles, repeating the desires, thanking and releasing the guardians and the entities who you wish to assist you; and, finally removing the circle.

Entities

The entities you will be using will be the Guardians of the North, South, East and West. You don't need a compass. Any direction which you designate as 'East' for instance becomes, for the purpose of your ritual, the East. You may also wish to invoke the assistance of your Planetary Angel, or your Holy Guardian Angel; or some other, non-physical entity. This is helped if you have the correct colour of candle but if not, ordinary white candles will suffice. The important thing is the intent and the degree of concentration used.

Why are coloured candles used?

Different colours have differing significances and attract differing types of influences. More than one colour of candle may be used at the same time. For instance, in addition to the basic candles you are using for the ritual, you may wish to have a third person represented. This can be done by representing them with a candle of the colour of their zodiacal sign. If you do not know their birth sign, then use a white candle. If you wish to influence any movement of attention, or desire towards, or away from you (or them), then move the requisite candle in the required direction as part of the rite.

Always use new, unused candles and let them burn down even if this means leaving them after the rite is completed. Prepare the candles by stroking them with firm strokes from the base to the tip, one direction only, while concentrating on what that particular candle is going to represent. The candle can be oiled in the same way with the requisite oil and, if you make your own candles, you can add the correct incense. Try to work *with*, not against the cosmic tides for the best results and do not use candle magic to affect harm to anyone.

Planetary Angels

AHAEL: Archangel of Venus, day is Friday.

Concerned with art, music, beauty, love.

ASARIEL:: Archangel of Neptune.

Rules maritime matters, clairvoyance, hidden things in life.

AZRAEL: Archangel of Pluto.
Rules buried treasure, mining, product dug from the Earth, death and after-life.
CASSIEL: Archangel of Saturn. Day Saturday.
Rules land, property and affects the elderly and racial destiny of humans.
GABRIEL: Archangel of the Moon. Day Monday.
Rules all concerned with women.
MICHAEL: Archangel of the Sun. Day Sunday.
Rules personal finance, career, ambition.
RAPHAEL: Archangel of Mercury. Day Wednesday.
Rules healing intellectual ability.
SACHIEL: Archangel of Jupiter. Day Thursday.
Rules gambling, gain of wealth, prestige.
SAMUEL: Archangel of Mars.
Rules machinery, physical violence, protects from fire.
URIEL: Archangel of Uranus.
Rules astrology, inspiration, sudden change and magical forces.

The colours of the planets are Venus–green; Saturn–black; Sun- gold; Mercury–orange; Jupiter–blue; mars- red.

The magical colours attributed to Earth, Moon, Neptune, Pluto and Uranus vary with differing schools of thought, e.g. Moon may be silver or purple. If in doubt, it is best to consult a reliable table of correspondences (i.e. *Liber 777*)

The Martial Arts

so often associated with Japan, or Nippon as it is more correctly called, are not originally or essentially Nipponese. In excess of 50 various forms exist all over the Far East. What has this to do with Western occultism?

Often a weapon is assumed to possess an individual *kami* or 'spirit' and this idea is not confined to the Far East. The Norse had a similar belief and named individual weapons such as swords and axes with names like 'Widow-maker' and 'Blood-drinker', etc.

The *naginata,* a long-handled, long-bladed pike-like weapon used by the Japanese and Chinese foot soldier was assumed to not only have an individual spirit, but also an 'over-spirit', a sort of Lord of the Naginata. If one thinks that the 18-foot spear used by the Scottish schiltrons and the foot-soldiers of Cromwell's day were awkward to handle, they would be amazed at the versatility with which a *naginata* can be handled by an expert. The hand-forged sword of the samurai, the *katana,* was also thought to contain the soul of its owner. Hence the reverence with which the genuine *katana* was handled by its owner and members of his family.

The *ninja,* so much and so inaccurately publicised in the West in recent years, had their own form of martial art known as *ninjutsu.* As with all Oriental 'physical' disciplines, beyond this is a form of *ninjutsu* that is associated with occult or 'higher level' practices. Few are the intrepid martial arts exponents who venture this far, for there is a great danger in its application.

This danger is the insidious influence and take-over of the practitioner by demons, evil *kami,* who gradually cease to be the servants of the practitioner and, instead, become his masters. These 'demons' are already lodged in the practitioner's subconscious mind before he commences his study of even the most basic martial arts practice. It is not the learning and practice of *ninjutsu* that releases these demons of the mind but its alliance with the higher-level of esoteric learning. The less acceptable 'personalities' of the practitioner are slowly unleashed and strengthened, building up their power and the confidence of the practitioner until he is convinced of his complete invincibility. This, of course, proves ultimately fatal.

Those occultists in the West who are interested in Japanese ways, though not necessarily in martial arts, may be subject to a similar danger if they are not careful in their behaviour and intentions. In either case, with the occult martial arts practitioner, or the occult non-martial arts practitioner, Eastern or Western, whoever fools with the Japanese *kami* system runs the risk of placing themselves in danger. The change is insidious. Occasionally it may even appear openly. It does not come as a divine or violent wind (*kamikazi*) - it comes as an imperceptible breeze (*not* god-like). The effect of such submission to negative *kami* is the same. The practitioner is piloting himself to suicide — a true, but not honourable, *kamikazi*.

Author's note: This article may seem to be a strange one but the interest in martial arts is great and though the ideas generally circulating about *ninja* are ludicrous, some occultists may combine an interest in Japanese matters with a lack of knowledge of the dangers of playing about with *kami*, which are more easily understood by the Japanese in the Japanese way. I suspect that in at least one case of *kami*-possession (allegedly confirmed independently by an occultist in another city), although the 'possessed' person had no great knowledge of martial arts (despite his claims), he didn't know how to handle my *katana* (which is an Italian replica, and not a genuine Japanese one).

Magic & Satanism

Is magic allowed in Satanism? Some of our christian brothers claim that all acts of magic are acts of the Devil, by whom they mean Satan. This being so, whenever they prepare the Communion by transmuting the wafer and the wine into Christ's body and blood, they are conducting a magical act — welcome to Christian-Satanists! In praying for rain they are hoping to cause a magical change in the weather. All are attempts to perform magic if only by invocation of the deity.

To be strictly correct, Satanism is a religious belief, just as witchcraft *can* be a religious belief (although ritual magic is not) — assuming that there is a difference between them. A religion is the worship of a deity, or a pantheon of such beings. Its essence is worship and devotion, whether the devotion is born of love or fear, e.g. "Thou hast free will, do as thou wilt, but if you don't do as I, thy God, say, then shall I kick thy ass."

Magic is not an act of devotion or worship It is an attempt to change the natural pattern of things by the imposition of Will. Magic is surely then not religion. Yet all religions are connected with, allied to and largely dependant on magic. In this respect, if it's good enough for everyone else, it's good enough for the Satanist of whichever path, from Benelist to the christian Dennis Wheatley-type.

Magic is the utilisation by Will of a neutral power. The power itself is neither good not evil. Such a distinction comes with the INTENT with which the power is manipulated. Even then good and evil are relative and largely dependent upon particular socio-religious mores which are themselves affected by, among other things, linear geographical and temporal subjects.

By all means then let those Satanists who wish to utilise magic do so, as do those Witches, Buddhists, Hebrews, Hindus, Muslims, christians, etc., who wish and are able to do so.

Rites of Passage

It is perhaps unfortunate that the term 'Rite of Passage' is assumed by so many to refer to the ceremonial which accompanies burial or cremation. Such ceremonies *are* Rites of Passage, but they are by no means the only ones. To understand fully we need to know just what is meant by the term. We need correct communication, otherwise inaccuracies will creep into 'understanding'. In this case, a veritable Babel of contradictory ideas may be generated for the future mystification of new students of the various occult systems.

Mankind is a creature of emotion, both in the personal and the group sense. Emotions affect and shape the behaviour of the individual, the family, the tribe, the nation, the race. They can cause different reactions in different people. They can be played upon like a musical instrument by orators and influential groups of people–thereby causing others to change their opinions and/or their course of action as a direct result. Emotion, then, has its place in Rites of Passage.

It is understood that the right hemisphere of the human brain is the one which is connected with intuition and emotion. There is no sign of this to be observed by the naked eye when a freshly exposed brain is examined *in situ.* Nor can anything be discerned when this hemisphere is dissected in thin slices. Scientific experimentation has, however, assured us that this right hemisphere is the side involved. Ritual is not in itself 'emotion' but it can affect emotion and, therefore it may be assumed to also have some connection with the right hemisphere of the human brain.

When a serious individual involves her/himself in a ritual, they are not normally co-operating merely in play or charade. If they are participating honestly in any form of ritual, they are making a form of statement to others. In a ritual that is performed alone, the celebrant is making a statement, not only to non-human entities but also to their own Inner Self.

As I have said, Rites of Passage are not always funerary ones. The 'Passage' is a transition from one state or stage to another. Thus we have the transition from childhood to adulthood; from apprentice to journeyman; from journeyman to master; from novice through the varying stages to Adept.

At each stage it is usual for a ceremony to take place, no matter how simple or elaborate it may be. With some, simplicity is the most effective but with others the more formality and ceremonial that is involved, the more satisfying they find it. The ceremony is not just an affirmation to those who are participating or observing. It is a means of impressing on the person's own psyche that a transition has come about, that a change has been effected, if not physically, then mentally or spiritually.

A passage has been made and has not been passed-by without notice. It has been accompanied by ritual, by ceremonial, no matter how trivial those transitions. Birthday parties are Rites of Passage, however wild or informal they may be; marriage is a passage from the state of being single to that of marriage and greater responsibility. Couples, on divorce, frequently celebrate their individual 'freedom' and the transition to the state of divorcee. The celebration is an emotional catharsis and is a true, though informal Rite of Passage.

Tan-Tricks

It is really surprising how many profess an interest in Tantra, only to have the interest swiftly evaporate if the opportunity to participate in the study of the subject presents itself. There are various levels, degrees and paths of Tantric study. To many, the term immediately calls to mind a vision of unlimited sexual activity in the guise of esoteric study.

For the benefit of the unenlightened, Tantric practices are *not* solely concerned with the chance, or the excuse to have a 'bit on the side'. It is true that in some varieties of Tantra there is a strong connection with Ophiolatria, though this is on different levels and for different purposes. Phallic worship, or of its representative, the serpent is spread throughout the world and in many cultures but some forms of Tantra have developed which are divorced, or at least separated from pure Ophidic systems. [Ophidian Current: The sexual energies used in connection with magical or mystical rites.] These systems tend to concentrate on mental control as well as physical and/or spiritual. Not all involve the necessity for training athletics or the practice of Hatha Yoga.

Nevertheless, athletic ability is an integral part of some Tantric rites as a lack of prowess may well result in an inguinal hernia. Admittedly such prowess is to ones advantage but there is far more to be hammered out and nailed down in the genuine pursuit of Tantric knowledge than mere 'screwing around'.

The Varma Marg group in India made a long-lasting impression on the renowned Madame Blavatsky, whose knowledge of the subject and its intension was perhaps as limited as her personal sexual experience. She may have had a diverse knowledge of numerology but in this case, for her 2+2=7 and, as a result, she had left a legacy of misunderstanding and dislike of the Varma Marg which persists to the present day.

One extremely interesting piece of writing among Bob's papers, however, was the nineteen hand-written pages of the first chapters of *The Book of Frater Asmodaeus.* This had been compiled as a series of numbered magical or philosophical 'truths' and obviously added to over a period of time, judging by the subtle changes in the handwriting.

Did Bob ever record this onto tape? There is no way of knowing but following his train of thought over making people think and view things from different perspectives and viewpoints, it may make for interesting reading along the same lines as Aleister Crowley's *Magic Without Tears.* To borrow a phrase or two from Louis Wilkinson who wrote of Crowley's work: "In some one phrase or other of *The Book* there is a direct message for every human being. The best way for the layman to approach this *Book* is to regard it as a letter written directly to himself. Even though he may not be able to understand some parts of the letter; he is sure to find other parts that are unmistakably addressed, in an intimately personal sense, to him."

Perhaps somewhere among these 'truths' the reader may find a passage that imparts a certain 'truth' that speaks directly to him or her.

The Book of Frater Asmodaeus

Templi Satanas Luciferi

The Templi Satanas Luciferi, the Church of Satan the Lightbearer, was officially consecrated on Walpurgis Eve, the 30th of April, 1987. This is exactly 21 years after the formation of the materialist Church of Satan by Anton Szandor LaVey. There are many points of agreement between the Church of Satan and the Church of Satan the Lightbearer. The *Templi Satanas Luciferi,* however, are not specifically anti-Christ.

They believe that the message that Emmanuel bar Joseph gave to the Jewish people was probably a good one but, as the Jews were not prepared to go against the established authority of the

Chief Rabbi to accept the teachings. Being very wary people by nature. (They even wanted the Ten Commandments in writing thereby causing Moses to nearly rupture himself carrying great tablets of stone down a mountain.)

The Apostles, assisted by the Greek-Jewish-Roman Saul of Tarsus, later St Paul, rearranged the teachings for the Gentiles. A much bigger market! Since then the teachings have been cut, pastes, subtracted from, added to, generally cobbled to suit so that the original only peeps out here and there. They are not against Christ but against the twisted teachings put out in His name.

Chapter One

The Almighty is everything, physical and non-physical, literally everything and therefore incomprehensible to our finite understanding. Being everything, the Almighty is male *and* female *and* neuter – not just a male entity. All things are created in the image of the Almighty because the Almighty is every part of every thing. The Almighty has no specific regard or concern for one species – i.e. mankind, among millions of species on one insignificant minor planet, in an outer arm of a spiral galaxy which is one among millions.

There are innumerable planes of existence on different levels in many dimensions of time and space. Mankind exists, physically, in one dimension of time and space. Mentally he can penetrate to other levels. Spiritually he can reach more levels. This is similar to a trained pearl or sponge diver being able to reach very much greater depths, for longer periods, than can the untrained diver–who can nevertheless, reach greater depths in safety than a non-swimmer.

As mankind can mentally and spiritually penetrate to other levels, so other entities can penetrate to our level, in our dimension. As not all men and women are benevolent, so not all intruding entities are benevolent. As men and women differ in intelligence, so do the entities of other planes.

Thus we have a variety of entities ranging from simple, uncomplicated 'elemental' entities to complex, powerful entities. As mankind wars on others of a different colour, culture or creed, so do entities of other levels war with each other. Just as mankind coerces other creatures to assist him (i.e. livestock) , so entities of other levels use humans to assist them in their inter-galactic, inter-dimensional and/or inter-planes struggles. Mankind seeks to improve his own chance in his struggles, by improving the training and development of the creatures assisting him. If he can influence the creatures of his opponents and teach them (by causing slight change in their training), to sabotage their master's aims, then this will be done.

These acts of 'sabotage' may have been directed at mankind by entities of other levels. We may be subject to 'disinformation'. Slight change made in information given to us result in slight influences to our mental processes, so that we ourselves not only sabotage the Earth but also indoctrinate our children to do the same.

Mankind lives his physical life on the planet, Earth. The Earth is subject to certain natural laws. These laws work in accordance with what we call 'Nature'. If mankind wishes to live in harmony with the Earth, he must live in accordance with Nature. Modern, 'civilised' man does not. Some of the 'civilised' religions appear to teach good actions but upon examination, there seems to be some inconsistency, some slight twisting of the truth. These religions often claim 'divine' or, in effect extra-terrestrial authority. Are the messages relaying this 'true' religious message from extra-terrestrial intelligences in harmony with the Earth, or are they from the enemies of Earth and Mankind?

If they are enemies, would they not seek to turn mankind against the true extra-terrestrial intelligences who are in harmony with the Earth? Has this been done? Have some humans been given knowledge by benevolent extra-terrestrials and tried to spread this knowledge, only to have later humans (under the influence of antagonistic extra-terrestrial intelligences), subtly change or add to the teachings?

Let us examine what evidence we have. First of all, for nearly 2,000 years the so-called 'developed world' has been controlled by a religion based on the alleged teaching of a man originally named Emmanuel, later to be given a name that was more acceptable in the Roman-controlled world of those days. A Greek name, in fact, because Greek culture was the 'in thing' just as everything American has been the 'in thing' since the last World War.

The teaching of Emmanuel included peace, love, helping others less fortunate, tolerance, lack of greed, etc., After 2,000 years what do we see? Rich vestments on archbishops, bishops, cardinals, etc., while some people of the same faith are reduced to buying second-hand clothes in jumbles sales, often held in church halls to swell the coffers of the church. The churches themselves, valuable buildings, often ornately decorated. Even the newer chapels and churches of the so-called Evangelists, although less well embellished are still costly. Yet their fellow men sleep in cardboard boxes under railway arches.

In the name of these teachings, they have exterminated whole sects of people, such as the Cathars, the Anabaptists and other Gnostic sects whose beliefs differed from their own. Killed men, women and children. The witches who also followed a different path were tortured, hanged or burnt. Even other christians were tortured and slaughtered; Catholic against Protestant.

Since the invention of gunpowder by the Chinese (who used it for fireworks), what has happened? Two christian friars, one English the other Austrian, brought gunpowder to christian Europe to be used for warfare. Since that time, every major weapon of mass destruction has been invented and developed by nominally christian nations.

In the name of progress the natural wealth of the Earth has been squandered on 'consumer goods' and weapons. The very environment is being affected by the cutting down of the rain forests; the damage to the ozone layer; the polluting of the air with noxious fumes, etc. One noticeable fact stands out. When the melt-down occurred at the Chernobyl atomic plant in Russia (where the christians do not control the state), the local population was evacuated.

In good, caring christian England, 30 years before Chernobyl, the plant at Sellafield (then called Windscale), had a melt-down that wasn't admitted for 30 years. How many people were evacuated? None! It was officially denied that there was never any danger. Are these the teachings of Emmanuel of Nazareth?

If not, where do we look for the followers of Emmanuel's *unchanged* parable teachings? Let us consider logically. If you twist and corrupt someone's teaching and gradually succeed in getting it accepted in an altered form, who do you most fear? Answer: those who try to live by the spirit of the original teaching. What do you do to combat these adversaries? Answer: include in the modified teachings, a hatred of such people and teach that they are evil, enemies of mankind, to be kept down or destroyed.

If the extra-terrestrial 'master' with its greater intelligence and knowledge puts this idea into the mind of the establishment, such concepts of hatred and persecution will be perpetuated. Fill the minds of people with stories of abomination.

The proof? You need none. Just spread the word, wherever possible via the media. Humans believe what is printed in newspapers, and books. Preach it from the pulpit and to hell with such precepts as "Judge not", "Love thy neighbour", "Cast first the beam from thine own eye,", etc.,

Before the solar, masculine cults gained the ascendancy, the concept of the Great Mother was supreme. The fear of the cult of the Mother Goddess again gaining popularity led to St Paul and the early church fathers recording such gems of Holy Doctrine as "Women are cess pits of evil", "Nests of vipers", "The gateway to hell". Natural sexual relations were an abomination, filthy, evil, etc., No wonder there are [still] few women priests in the christian churches.

[What are the most common questions that people ask about Satanism? Here Bob addresses some of the more serious aspects of modern, so-called Satanists.]

Do Satanists sacrifice animals, etc?
Unfortunately, some who would like to *call* themselves Satanists appear to have done so.

Should all Satanists be assumed to carry out such acts?
No more surely than because a percentage of Christian ministers have a penchant for chasing choirboys and boy scouts, and fondling schoolgirls; or because the Roman Catholic church, having in the past castrated young boys to preserve their voices for the Papal Choir, should the whole Christian movement be stigmatised.

Why do those calling themselves Satanists do such things?
Because they have read this is what Satanists do and how they behave.

Where have they read such things?
Not in any *Satanic Bible* purporting to be the true word of the Lord of the World. No! They have read it in the works of the early Christian fathers and in the imaginative writings of authors such as the late Dennis Wheatley.

Why do the Luciferians accept the name 'Satanists'?
According to the early Hebrew writings, *satans* (plural you notice, not singular), were sons of God employed by God to observe and bear witness to the wrong-doings of man. The meaning of the word *satan* is adversary. Not enemy. Is prosecuting council, or a witness for the prosecution an inveterate enemy of the accused person? They are his adversaries only.

Luciferians, followers of Lucifer the Lightbearer, are adversaries of those who despoil the Earth and destroy life, mankind included. They are thus the adversaries, NOT of Emmanuel of Nazareth but of those who have twisted his alleged teachings, built up money-spinning wealth and power-collecting organisations in his name and who, in his name, persecuting and harassing those who seek to confirm to natural ways and live with, not on, the Earth.

As adversaries of those who inculcate the message of hate, judgement and intolerance into children from birth (even in school, enforcing their teaching by law), the followers of Lucifer, Lord of this world, as the personification of the male principle, and of the Great Mother, as personification of the female principle, are honoured to be called Satanists, or adversaries.

Would you ask the Rev Ian Paisley for an unbiased idea of the beliefs of the Roman Catholic Church; or the Pope for an unbiased idea of Communism; an ex-SS General for the beliefs of Judaism; or an extreme Zionist for an unbiased view on the right of the Palestinians? Would you believe any such views if given without question or clarification? Yet how many otherwise discerning people blindly accept the rabid ranting about Satanists? If you accept these, then accept that women are evil, cess-pits of corruption. Relegate women to the roles of mindless chattels, the personal property of their men-folk, slaves for a man to do with as he will.

For the Luciferians, the sexes are equal, as the male and female principles, representing the Almighty in this small world, in this particular plane, dimension, time and space are equal. If they are merely extra-terrestrials with superior intelligence, given charge of this world and fighting other entities who seek to despoil it, then so be it! Better to assist such beings as adversaries, or *satans,* of the despoilers, powerful as they may be.

The Lord and Lady of this world do not threaten you with punishments often death, or promise paradise for eternity for doing their will. They do not ask that you let them take over your mind, your spirit you body in abject surrender to become a slave of your own volition to another entity professing to have your best interests at heart. The Luciferian is free to question; free to think; free to accept or reject with no fear of retribution from a mighty entity which is so fearful as to punish a simple, weak, human being who dares to think for itself.

Are Witches Satanists?

The Christain church says they are and often the Christian church is truthful, especially when the truth serves its purpose, as happens here. If Witches are Satanists (i.e. adversaries of the despoilers) then they must be evil and must be stamped out! Unfortunately, a large proportion of modern Witches, still affected by childhood training and Dennis Wheatley-type stories, disagree.

They have come across, in Wicca, as something good, whole-some and natural. So they seek to disassociate themselves from Satanism. They refuse to see their 'Horned God of Nature' as the Lord of this World; adversary or *satan,* of the world's despoilers. And in this they assist the despoilers becoming the unwitting allies of those who, given the chance, will destroy them and their world.

Are Satanists Witches?
Not all? Witches, especially those of Old Craft are what they are by token of their natural ability.

Is there an anti-Christ?
The anti-Christ is the Great Entity, the extra-terrestrial intelligence who is opposed to life on Earth and the spiritual progression of mankind. In no way then can Lucifer, the Lightbringer (light = knowledge, wisdom and understanding), *satan* and 'devil' of the Christian church, be the anti-Christ, opposing himself. Luciferians accept the teaching of Emmanuel of Nazareth. They cannot accept the Greek-named puppet-image set up in his place by the servants of the Great Enemy.

These unwitting servants, having given themselves over to the Great Enemy's control, lie, twist and deceive yet they are voluble in protesting that it is the Lord of this World who is the deceiver. As the Buddha says: "All is illusion!" What we see are reflections and reflections are REVERSED images.

When you realise you are looking in a mirror, your mind can rationalise the truth. Luciferians and Satanists may appear to be against Emmanuel of Nazareth. But those few who dare to open themselves to retribution in an attempt to cause men and women to think for themselves, point out the inconsistencies in what mankind is expected and encouraged to accept as 'gospel' and the Word of God.

Chapter Two
Wicca or Witchcraft, the Craft of the Wise, is said to be a very old religion. As a fertility religion it may claim to be so, but as to the modern rites and ceremonies dating back to the Stone Age, I have strong doubts. The *Book of Shadows* so beloved of modern day Witches is basically the Witches' equivalent of the magician's *grimoire,* a handy notebook of information for personal reference.

Did medieval Witches have *Books of Shadows*?
Not unless they could read and since few of the nobility could, let alone the village wise woman.

Did covens of 13 meeting regularly?
Hardly in medieval times, surely? Villagers, especially the women, often lived their entire lives in an area of a few square miles, going no further than the nearest market town.

Most people, up at dawn, were in bed soon after sunset and unlikely to go traipsing off every month, along unlit rough tracks for a night's celebration. Worship would be a private concern, especially with the church's condemnation of other beliefs.

This historical pouring of cold water does not detract from the authenticity of Old Craft. No matter how much is traditional British, or Celtic, or Greek, or Egyptian in the pagan rites practised by any sect today, they are entitled to call themselves pagan if they wish. What matters is the sincerity of intention. That rites and ceremonies are not original is of no great concern. All things have to change or they stagnate and decay.

It is the underlying faith which matters and the sincerity with which the faith is symbolised. As long as the witch respects Nature or natural ways, understanding the fundamental idea of a positive and negative principle, symbolised as male *and* female, God *and* Goddess, Lord *and* Lady, as representatives of a greater principle of which everything is a part, it matters not what particular path they follow. All paths are equal in the Great Work.

There are, however, some basic differences between those Wiccans and pagans who are Luciferian and those who are not.

One difference, already mentioned, is that the non-Luciferian Wiccan/pagan denies any connection with the Lord of this World, as Lucifer, the bearer of the Light of Knowledge, Wisdom and Understanding.

Some mistakenly think that this may allow them to ingratiate themselves with the anti-Satanic Christians and will show Wicca and/or paganism in a better light to the general brain-washed public. Given the right circumstances they, for all their denials, will again hang as high and burn as fiercely as Satanists.

A second difference is connected to the first. The non-Luciferian pagan is often intolerant. This shows not only in their judging of Satanism as evil, without knowledge of the subject, but too frequently such Wiccans and pagans look askance at those on other paths and are not ready to accept the ways of others as valid pagan paths.

A third difference is that many non-Luciferian Wiccans/pagans accept the Goddess as the Be All & End All of the Craft, demoting the God to the role of a deified gigolo, a holy 'toy boy', or a sort of superior servant, who dances attendance on the Goddess.

This may be a natural reaction after centuries of male domination. It is noticeable that to the Dennis Wheatley following, anti-social behaviour shows that the Goddess is nothing and the females are quite often of only auxiliary importance, though exceptions do occur.

A fourth difference may be found in the Wiccan Rede. To the Gardnerian, Alexandrian and some other Wiccan sects this is: "An ye harm none—do as ye will". We will forget shall we, the way so many who profess to follow this Rede, harm the reputation of Satanists and those of other paths by their judgements, often lacking understanding and by their criticisms. Alleged 'hereditary' witches for example, say Alexandrians are not true witches, to use but one example.

The Luciferian witch tries to follow this Wiccan Rede generally but with the proviso, "As long as none seek to harm you". The Luciferian will turn the other cheek, may do so repeatedly, but not for too long. If the soft answer fails to turn away wrath, then let the mailed fist instil respect through fear. Remember those who have gone before to the torture chamber, the gallows or the stake.

Why is it that some cannot see that the God and Goddess, Lord and Lady, Male and Female are, though distinctive in their own right, merely different aspects of one Whole?
The reason is in our imperfect understanding. If you pass by a building site which is surrounded by a fence which has the occasional crack in it, you can look through each crack in turn to see the activity on the site.

Through one crack you may see a man mixing sand, cement and water. Through another a man wheeling a barrow filled with what looks like liquid mud. The view through the third crack shows a man carrying bricks in a hod, while through a forth you see a bricklayer using the bricks and mortar brought in the barrow to build a wall.

With your adult knowledge you can relate the four scenes and know what is going on. Let a child of 3 or 4 years of age look through the cracks and see the same scenes, and they will be incomprehensible to him or her. They have not the knowledge to evaluate the things they see. Mankind is similarly lacking in knowledge to varying degrees.

The Mystical Mug Exercise

Pick up an ordinary drinking mug. Imagine that the mug is floating in front of you, at eye level, the handle standing out to the left. Imagine now that you are describing EXACTLY what you see to a blind person.

What do you actually see? Assume you have never seen a mug before, it is a strange and wonderful phenomena. You would say you saw a roughly square or rectangular object but perhaps tapering slightly towards the base.

It appeared to be convex towards you. Standing out to the left a curved projection, joining the main body just below the top and about 2/3 of the way down the body. You describe the colour and decorative pattern if any. Sex? If it has any it must be male, because of the projection.

The blind man then has the mug described to him by someone seeing it from 90 degrees to the right of the first observer. Same general shape, colour and pattern but no projection. It must be similar but not the same. Sex? No projection, can't be male. No hollows, can't be female. It might therefore be neuter.

He then has it described to him by someone viewing directly from above. Basic shape now circular, apparently mainly tubular or cylindrical, flat at the end. A single stem projection jutting out from the main body. The top of the handle covers the rest from view. Same colour but no decorative pattern. It cannot be related to the first or second object at all. Sex? Projection indicates male, hollow cylinder indicates female, might be hermaphroditic.

If the mug were described by people viewing separately from top, bottom and four sides, let alone at oblique angles, the blind man would assume they were seeing several objects, some of which may or may not be related.

If each viewer described what he saw to an outsider who had not seen the object, none of these people would believe the others had only described a different view of the same object.

Someone familiar with a mug might realise, but even then the description, if it could be evaluated by those who had never seen one, would not convey what it was made from, how it was constructed, fired, decorated, glazed–or even what its purpose was.

Humans visualise or have described to them various entities which they call male Gods, female Goddesses, hermaphrodites like Baphomet, neuters like seraphim, angels, demons, etc. All are parts of the Whole. With the mug, the container-part has one purpose, its handle another. So have the different entities different purposes.

We used for this example of selective angles of view, a simple mug. How much more complicated would I have been to use and describe from different angles–a typewriter? The more complex the subject, the harder to understand the nature and purpose. Yet men and women are ready to make judgements from the information gained from limited viewing, restricted angles and totally inadequate knowledge. On similar judgements they condemn those with other beliefs.

The Luciferian then is an adversary of these who appear to be destroying the Earth but is ready to be convinced otherwise. The Luciferian will, if necessary, defend him or herself, and tries not to judge harshly those who follow other paths.

Was Emmanuel of Nazareth one view, one angle of the Light-bearer of which Satan-Lucifer is another and Cernunnous, Pan, Isis, Aphrodite, Venus, Horus, etc., other views from different angles? Before we act against those with different views let us give them the opportunity to leave us to our beliefs in peace.

A new age is dawning for mankind. Let it be an age of understanding. It may be too late for the older witches, especially those High Priests and High Priestesses who have been practising for decades, whitewashing the Craft by accepting without thought or question the induced, age-old view that Satan is the Lord of Evil. Such will continue in their ignorance of understanding, to try to dis-associate themselves from the whole idea of Satanism.

So be it! They are no longer young. Their influence will give way to that of younger, less constrained minds, those prepared to reason, to accept if not the teachings at least the sincerity of those of other paths.

For the simple minds which like an easy pleasant belief with obvious results, for only a little expenditure of thought or study there will still exist the forms of the Craft as we know them today. For those who need to reason, to think, to question, the Craft will progress, will grow and will change as the caterpillar changes into a butterfly. There are those who nurtured the seeds laid by the previous generations; others took cuttings from the growing plants and caused the hybrid to evolve further. Some have planted new seeds which may transform the Craft completely.

Certain those people and others have had contact with extra-terrestrial intelligences, be they termed angels, devils, demons, demi-gods or visitors from time and space. The messages received by these people at first sight may frequently appear to be contradictory. Time may show that they are not. That it is our present, poor level of understanding which is responsible for the apparent discrepancies. They may be but different views of the same object, like the different appearances of the mug, seen from different angles.

In time all could be revealed in totality. But have we the time? A new age is dawning but it is one which could bring the downfall of mankind and much of life on this planet.

The last decade of this century [20th] will see which decision mankind will make. Whether he will allow his materialism or his spiritual awareness to conquer. The loss of the human body is nothing in one respect. The spirit or spirits continue to exist though the body appears to be destroyed. *Appears* to be destroyed because, in reality, nothing can be completely destroyed—only changed in form. That is why there is no such thing as a 'new soul'. Or a 'new life'. All that occurs is that the spirit evolves or degenerates, it tales one path of another and is continually given a new vehicle or body to control.

There is this constant interplay in life on countless planes, levels, dimensions and universes. All is life and if spiritual advance is to be gained, this basic fact must be realised in its entirety. Titles, positions, rank, social standing are all crutches for the ego and meaningless in the greater concept. The terms Witch King Witch, Witch Queen, High Priest, High Priestess, Adept, Master, Guru, Sage, Rabbi, etc., are of temporary use only and only for those who need to see people bear such titles before they will give credence to what such people say. The one bearing such a title who feels the need to bear it, feeds his or her own ego and is devoid of understanding if not of knowledge.

[According to Bob's notes, there should have been another two chapters – originally written as the script for tapes—but to date these have not be found either in written or taped form.]

Coven of the Scales

In the first issue of *Moebius Trip* (1993) an article entitled 'Solitaire' appeared, written by Bob, that made public, details of the Coven of the Scales for the first time.

There are Pagans and there are plastic Pagans, Shamans and sham shamans, mini-magicians and genuine article, oriental and occidental Ophidians, Witches of all kinds. All to one degree or another, students and/or practitioners of the occult. There are some who call themselves 'Masters' but these show by their claims their low level of development and knowledge.

By this criticism I infer only those who *claim* mastery of the occult in any particular branch, not those who attain a particular grade, degree or distinction which incorporated the title, as in *Magister Templi*, Master of the Temple or *Magister Daemonae*, Demon Master, (though this is more correctly master of spirits).

Degrees, grades and distinctions, where not self-granted, are bestowed by a Coven, Order, Group, Scale, Ring, Lodge, Circle or some other organised body. There are many occultists who hold that membership of an organisation is essential; that otherwise 'training' cannot be acquired. To some extent this was true fifty years ago when witchcraft was illegal and anyone attempting to obtain a book on occult subjects was likely to be looked at somewhat askance.

Training in an organisation meant imbibing, not questioning, that which you were taught. Rebellious, independent thoughts might be held but were rarely voiced. The result was in some organisations stifling and containing. Development was on ordered and fixed lines with well defined parameters. But evolution is not to be stopped and some of us did develop independent, if surreptitious ideas.

The occult Renaissance probably commenced, at least in Britain, with the repeal of the Witchcraft Act. The lock gates of witchcraft were opened slightly, then forced back by Gardner & Sanders. Books on all forms of occult knowledge were written.

Some, indeed many, are pure rip-offs but others have much to offer. The old *grimoires* were superseded. No longer did one have to carefully read between the lines to glean grains of gold and silver from the mass of literary excreta. There was still some excreta but the proportion, in relation to nourishment, was less.

Occult organisations sprung up like mushrooms in this new dawn of paganism. Dangerous spiritual toadstools also sprang up and continue to do so with the advent of the occult con-men, the charming, smooth talking charlatans. It seemed that the Golden Dawn of organised occultism was breaking. The availability of informative books; the onslaught of the media and its masters; the wealthy and biased religious organisations.

Not to mention the fuelling of those fears placed in the minds of the accepting, unthinking, zombie section of the public by generations of propaganda. These were factors which caused many, even those with membership of and formal training by occult organisations, to retire from the limelight and practice alone or with only one or two trusted companions.

It might seem that, as every individual's path differs (if only infinitesimally), from everyone else's, that the next stage of development is that of the lone Witch, the solo Magician, etc. – i.e. the Solitaire. All practicing alone with little or no contact with others of the same broad path, let alone of a different discipline. This state has the advantage of privacy in personal spiritual advancement with less chance of one's religious beliefs becoming known, perhaps making one a target, as a loner, for team-handed bigots. But there are disadvantages.

Solitary working can lead to sterility of thought, with only books to stimulate the mind. When, not if, there arises that dread spectre, 'The Dark Night of the Soul', it must be faced alone, faced and conquered or submitted to, with its subsequent spiritual regression. It comes to all who spiritually progress and each failed attack strengthens your defences; but a first, second or third attack can, for a truly solo practitioner, be disastrous, even fatal. The coroner may claim suicide by reason of depression but the true cause may be the facing, truly alone, of a 'Dark Night of the Soul'.

How may the Solitaire stay solo yet have support and help when needed? The Solitaire may join an organisation and cease to be a Solitaire, accepting the group's ideas and beliefs - subjecting their own. They may join a Federation or a Fellowship as an individual member which may afford them contact with someone to turn to if they can withstand the first attack long enough to take advantage of the Royal Mail.

The third option is for the solitary worker to join a multi-path 'coven'. As the term implies, the original idea was for such organisations to be for Witches of all paths. The term coven, from the Scots-Gaelic *cuveen,* means 'a group of association' and is thus only connected with witchcraft by traditional usage. The scope of the true multi-path coven has changed or developed beyond the restrictions of application only to Witches.

If we take, for example, the Coven of the Scales, these changes will be apparent. The Coven of the Scales was formed for balance, as the name implies; also to remove the 'scales' from the eyes of biased occultists. It took the place of the Coven of Saira & Neqron, that had replaced the Moonraker Coven which, with its hived-off covens was persecuted and driven underground in the 1960s.

Originally a form of traditional coven, it adopted, in the early sixties, the degree system of the Gardnerian system, as it had already adopted many non-Witchcraft magical additions. As a result, the Coven of the Scales appears now totally unrecognisable from the Moonraker Coven and its satellite covens. Now, coven members do not live within easy visiting distance of each other; they do not join together in one group for the festivals. They do not all follow one path. This coven is composed mainly of solitary workers of various paths. Non-Witches are not exempt from membership providing they are occultist.

So-called 'teaching' is given by letter or tape in which suggestions are made in order to give rise to thought. Not standard items of belief, they are simply intended to *provoke thought.* The member has the brain stimulated in a way that does not easily occur where training involves spoon-feeding with 'what must be believed'. Understanding has to be worked for ... but questions *can* be asked; and the answers may give rise to totally different possible answers. No matter! The member thinks for themselves. They are responsible for their own progress on their own individual path..

Those members who want contact with others holding similar views and ideas are put in touch with each other, initially if required via a box number. A listening ear is available when the 'Dark Night of the Soul' strikes, or the lifting of the veils occur.

Psychologically such an organisation has an advantage for the member, who remains a Solitaire, independent, progressing at their own speed, responsible for and to themselves, but at the same time part of a distinct group. The leaders of the group, like God in the christian prayer, "An ever present help in the time of trouble". Like skirmishers by the occult battlefield, members, though alone, know that they have backup when needed.

This multi-path way might be the way in which the occult shall evolve to cause genuine respect and understanding between practitioners of different systems and differing branches of the same system. The way in which both groups and solo practitioners may work together in mutual respect.

Alastair R. Clay-Egerton 20th. Feb.1993

[The Coven of the Scales is still operational and would welcome contact by any of the old Moonraker members or former members of Bob and Mériém's groups. It has since discarded the 'Garderian three degree' system and returned to an intense period of study followed by formal Initiation. It also remains a multi-path organisation and only open to those who have undergone the prescribed training which is recognised and accepted by the Elders of the Coven of the Scales.]

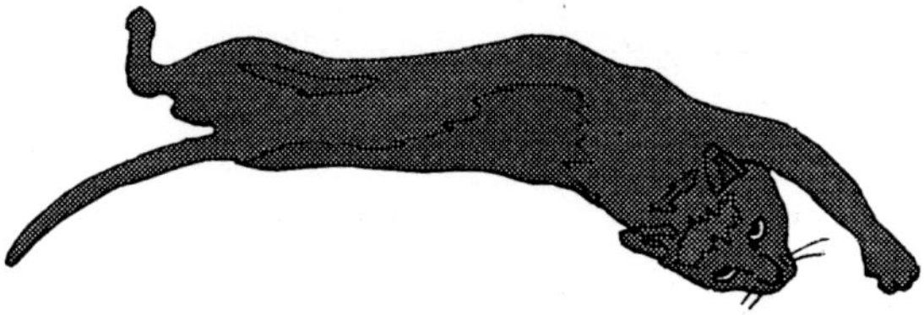

Tripod

In going through all the paperwork, there was an article titled, 'Tutelary Animals' which was a realistic and objective account of losing a pet and obviously intended for publication as a comfort to others who found themselves in a similar situation. There was also an earlier piece, written immediately after Tripod, Bob and Mériém's cat had died, dated 4th November 1993

Which way to go?

Include the final piece, to illustrate the practical view of "All things must pass" - or the earlier one, that showed old Asmodaeus, scourge of the posing classes, up for the old pussy cat he really was? Sorry Bob, it had to be the latter.

"Black furred one, we prepared a bed in an enclosed den for your feral mother to give you and your siblings birth. We saw you introduced to the outside world and watched you play. You had no name other than 'one of the black ones'. The Great Mother has many ways to entwine the fates of her creatures and if Her way with you seemed cruel, I hope that it had its later compensations.

The Alsatian that savaged a small kitten can be forgiven. Its master had trained it to kill cats. The fault and the atonement in another plane is his, not so much his dogs. Perchance he and his dog were used by the Great Mother to bring us closer together. Who are we to say? It is beyond us to see all.

When you disappeared we thought you had been taken away by children. By the time you were discovered where you had crawled to die, the gangrene was extensive. The vet would have put you to sleep as you had no home, and if she amputated your leg from the hip, no chance of survival alone. That we offered you a home if you survived an operation was not in remembrance of my fifty-first birthday, or because we cared for you anymore than any other animal. I am no stranger to bringing swift death to the Lady's creatures, especially when badly injured or terminally and painfully sick. A cat with three legs would be a great talking point and an obvious familiar for Witches. This must have been the reason for my not painlessly interrupting the flow in your jugular—pure selfishness on my part. Mériém would have preferred you to have a chance anyway.

The vet asked what your name was for her records. You had none, so I told her that if you survived the operation you would be called Tripod. As you would have three legs only. You survived but the vet said you would not have a long life, the osteonecrosis was the worst she had seen. You joined the family, Mériém, myself and the two other ex-ferals, Old Mr Pickwick and Tabitha Lady—you joined the race to see which of us would outlast the others.

The Great Mother took back Tabitha about six and a half years ago; paralysed to the neck, she died in Mériém's arms. A year later Mr Pickwick jumped from my knee and suffered a stroke, affecting his left side, like me. His heart gave out a few hours later. You were left in the race with us. I will always remember you trying to wake Mr Pickwick up and trying to pull him to his feet. Liberties you would not normally have taken with that Victor Meldrew of the feline world.

I nearly beat you to it. Six months ago when I was taken to the coronary care unit but I survived to do a Group 4 and escape. In my absence you took over the leadership as the 'man of the house'. You did not search for me for as long as you had when I too had had an operation for gangrene. Perhaps you remembered and knew I would come back. Did you think 'Big Man' was hunting chick or tuna for 'Little Man'?

We knew when you went to ground under my bed for a week, eating only a little every two days that you were going to leave us. I was already awake when you started to howl just after midnight. There was no disrespect meant in pulling you out and carrying you downstairs to where Mériém was in bed. After I had made a bed on the floor by Mériém;'s bed and let you lie across my arm you quietened, except for a couple of wails in the early hours. It was obviously your heart and I know the pain well. In the morning, while I had breakfast, you lay on Mériém's arm, licked her hand as you had mine and put your front paws around her neck. At half past 12 noon, the day before my 63rd birthday, you had a last violent heart spasm. Your breathing slowed in your coma and at 12.40 pm you left us after 12 years. You had never been smacked in that time, though on rare occasions you merited it. You did not chase birds and had insisted on the birds being fed before you would eat in the mornings.

You showed great tolerance of other creatures with the exception of moths and crane flies if they invaded the house. Mice you licked before bringing them to be dried off and released outside. If only humans could learn from you. I have not wept for you little brother; I did not weep for my children when I buried them, or at their death. Emotions I was brought up to hide. It is not that I have no feelings, just that I do not put them on show for others.

During your last week and since your death I have not, as Asmodaeus, put pen to paper. No articles, no letters, no tapes even. Humour has not died with you but it is taking a rest.

We do not rail against the Goddess for taking you. We give her thanks for that 12 years we knew you and learned from you. Patience in adversity and suffering, personal independence though one of a group. Tolerance of others, quietness, dignified affection. The Goddess used you as a tutor in these things. Mankind looks upon animals as inferior beings. The Goddess makes use of such as you to gently put us in our place.

Be blessed of the Goddess, Tripod. May she grant us the honour in time, of encountering you again.

Conclusion

Although Bob Clay-Egerton was an accomplished Witch and Ritual Magician, he had no affiliation with any of the famous magical Orders such as the Hermetic Order of the Golden Dawn or the *Ordo Templi Orientis* (OTO). His reason being that he often felt their rigid degree structure could often be detrimental to magical advancement. His teaching methods were those of a strict disciplinarian in terms of occult Source and Science but he had an almost Puckish delight in the free-fall experimentation that he encouraged in his students. He was nevertheless always there to bail you out of trouble, sure in the knowledge that the same mistake would not be made twice – the lesson having been well learnt.

There are those claiming some line of descent from his Tradition; all we would say is, that as a Witch or Magus is 'known by their work and their silence' those magical outpourings now in the public domain merely demonstrate that there is no substance to the shadow.

Bob actively loathed those 'posturing poltroons' who denigrated the name of occultism *per se* and, as his writings will have shown, was not adverse to exposing and ridiculing the ignorance and bigotry that often surfaces in paganism. Whilst not suffering fools gladly, it was a constant source of delight to him if his verbal bludgeoning made people stop and think ... and question.

Hopefully, these collected writings of Alastair 'Bob' Clay-Egerton *will* strike a responsive chord in someone's mind. That they may cause someone to think for themselves, instead of being influenced by the large amount of misinformation that is prevalent in today's occult teaching

MD

Index

Other titles from ignotus press

13 Moons—Fiona Walker-Craven
Creative Pathways—Suzanne Ruthven
What You Call Time- Suzanne Ruthven
Malleus Satani—Suzanne Ruthven
Whittlewood-Suzanne Ruthven
Coarse Witchcraft—Rupert & Gabrielle Percy
Hearth & Garden -Gabrielle Sidonie
The Hollow Tree-Mélusine Draco
The Thelemic Handbook-Mélusine Draco
Liber Ægyptius-Mélusine Draco
Egyptian Book of Days-Mélusine Draco
Root & Branch- Draco & Harriss
A Witch's Treasury of the Countryside
Draco & Harriss
Rites of Shadow-E A St George
High Rise Witch—Fiona Walker-Craven

Website: www.ignotuspress.com

A R Clay-Egerton